FINDING YOUR WAY

through

Domestic Abuse

Finding Your Way through Domestic Abuse is full of many important perspectives about intimate partner violence. Connie Fourré raises many important points to think about, particularly for those who might be new to the field of domestic violence. This book will help enlighten those who work with both batterers and survivors.

Dave Mathews
Director of Therapy, The Domestic Abuse Project,
Minneapolis, Minnesota

Connie Fourré knows our experience—she has lived it. She "gets" why we stay. She names the pain and the grief of leaving. She confronts the truth of danger to our bodies and souls. And she dares us to believe that healing can truly happen, recovery can bring new life, and happiness can be ours. She guides us along the way with wisdom, honesty, and faith.

Elizabeth Andress
survivor

FINDING YOUR WAY

through

Domestic Abuse

A Guide to Physical, Emotional, and Spiritual Healing

Connie Fourré

ave maria press AMP notre dame, indiana

Founded in 1865, Ave Maria Press is a ministry of the Indiana Province of Holy Cross.

www.avemariapress.com

ISBN-10 1-59471-076-7   ISBN-13 978-1-59471-076-6

Cover and text design by Brian C. Conley

Printed and bound in the United States of America.

Library of Congress Cataloging-in-Publication Data is available

*From the bottom of my heart, I want to thank
my sister, Kate Bally,
my friend, Holly Hoey Germann,
and my therapist, Laura Helling-Christy.
Without them I might never have reached the sunlight.*

*This book is dedicated to my children
and to all who spend time in the shadow of abuse,
yet learn to flourish.*

Contents

Preface

This book is written for anyone recovering from a relationship with an abusive partner. These pages apply equally to women who have experienced intense physical abuse and to those who have endured emotional abuse. All forms of abuse leave deep wounds, and this book is designed to help survivors heal and move forward into a new and better life.

There are excellent books available dealing with the practical and legal aspects of leaving an abusive relationship and I strongly recommend the materials listed in the resources section, but this book focuses more on the internal reality of abuse and its effects. It is also written most clearly for women who are considering ending or who have decided to end, their relationship. This is not in any way a judgment on women who choose to stay. I stayed in my marriage for twenty-four years, hoping that someday things would change for the better. These pages reflect my understanding that comes from those years as well as my continued growth since.

As you read these pages you may think, "So many women have endured much worse abuse than I have." You may see photos of women in the Middle East imprisoned in burquas and suffering unimaginable oppression, and your mind goes numb. Thousands of women in this country endure daily beatings and torture that rival the most brutal prisons in the world. But as my therapist often reminded my recovery group, "It's not a contest." Abuse is not a contest. It does not matter that another woman's experience is different from or worse than yours any more than it would matter if someone else's cancer were "worse" than yours. Abuse is abuse, and it is always damaging. No one deserves to be abused—ever. Everyone who is a target of abuse deserves support and the resources needed to recover.

I cannot speak as a therapist or someone with extensive formal training in psychology. I speak as a woman who for more than twenty years searched intently for help to understand and cope with my experience and its effect on my children. For fifteen years I have taught a high school human relations course, and when I added a unit on domestic abuse I could see in my students' eyes that I was naming a reality some knew all too well. My qualifications are that I am a survivor, a writer, an educator, a mother, a volunteer, and a human being.

I would never have signed up for this journey. Frankly, given the chance, I would opt out of whatever challenges lie ahead. Yet now that I have finally gotten my feet on a safe shore, I realize there has been blessing along the way. Like Maya Angelou, I have discovered, to my surprise, that I "wouldn't take nothin' for my journey now."[1] I have wisdom and strength that I could not possibly have learned any other way. I have been healed from a pain that began long before I met my former husband. Miraculously, in many ways I am more intact as a human being now than I was when my marriage began, although there are areas of myself that will forever remain vulnerable.

I have not found any one program or theory that thoroughly explains the experiences that mystified me over the years. This book is my synthesis, drawn from four primary sources: my own experience and the stories I have heard and read, abuser and survivor recovery programs, insight from the chemical dependency field, and the wisdom of Mahatma Gandhi and Martin Luther King, Jr., on responding to violence and hatred. My approach is shaped by my reliance on spirituality to gain strength and guidance for my life.

My hope is that my search and struggle can shed some light on the path for other women whose lives and families are touched by the tragedy of abuse. The way out of the storm of abuse is frightening and painful. But wherever you are today, your life *can* be better—much better.

Introduction

"I can't believe I'm here."

Every abused woman has murmured these words to herself. They sound in her heart as she endures a barrage of insults or slowly picks herself up after yet another physical assault. They echo again as she finds herself in a divorce court, recovery group, or hospital emergency room. Shock and disbelief are normal responses to any event that violates the core of a woman's dignity and safety as a human being.

Abuse and violence are both so devastating that being targeted, especially by a beloved partner, shakes a woman's sense of reality. Women who grew up in abusive families are astonished to find themselves in the same predicament they vowed to escape. Women raised in loving homes cannot understand how a phenomenon so foreign and so terrible could possibly have entered and taken over their world.

Domestic abuse and violence take an appalling toll in the United States and worldwide. Intimate partners kill 1,500 women every year in America, and untold thousands die internationally at the hands of those pledged to care for them.[2] Despairing women take their own lives—fatalities that are never attributed to their real cause. These deaths are the tip of the iceberg; unimaginable damage is also done to women who survive years of physical, sexual, and emotional assault. Vulnerable children who witness and are marked by this trauma bear their own wounds and carry the syndrome into the next generation.

Domestic abuse is a secret still locked in the closet, buried in the same silence and shame that cloaked alcoholism not too many years ago. Although the Surgeon General has labeled domestic violence a public health crisis, the topic is rarely mentioned in school health classes. Students who are thoroughly instructed on symptoms of depression, chemical dependency, and sexually transmitted diseases learn nothing about a syndrome that annually brings one million American women to physicians and emergency rooms for treatment.[3] Parents who openly express concern about the dangers of drugs and alcohol for their children live in staunch denial that intimate violence exists in their communities.

A public information session on domestic abuse rarely draws a large crowd. Most people are uncomfortable with the issue and unaware of its magnitude. Those who are caught in an abusive relationship often have trouble naming the abuse to themselves and are ashamed to be publicly associated with the issue. For this and many other important reasons, domestic abuse continues to wreak havoc in hundreds of thousands of homes across America, while its dark legacy passes silently from one generation to the next.

Over the last twenty-five years men and women across the country have developed treatment programs for abusers and recovery programs and shelters to help women and children. People of courage and compassion work with perpetrators and survivors to heal the damage and teach new strategies for developing healthy relationships. A number of excellent books on the topic are now available, and police and court systems are gradually becoming more responsive. While many women are still without resources, very real progress has been made.

These efforts leave many untouched, however. Thousands of families are haunted by a pattern of anger and abuse that never quite crosses the threshold to physical assault. The behavior that becomes so familiar and predictable to them is never called by its real name. This form of abuse leaves no physical mark on its victims, but the psychic damage is devastating.

When clear physical violence is not present, many women spend years struggling to give themselves permission to leave a marriage. Understanding and support from friends, family, and the professional community can be very hard to come by.

CLARIFYING TERMS

When speaking of abuse it is important to be careful with language. Clear language promotes clear thinking, and abused women need clarity in order to recover. The following working definitions will be used throughout this book.

Research indicates that 95 percent of serious domestic assault is committed by men against women. While domestic abuse perpetrated by women is underreported because of the shame attached to men who experience it, homicide statistics are a fairly accurate indicator of gender dynamics: It is rare for a woman to kill a male partner unless a pattern of assault by the male is present in the relationship.

Because of men's greater physical strength and the socialization of men toward aggression and women toward submission and caretaking (and therefore the potential for sexual assault), male violence toward women generally carries greater impact than the reverse. When I ask my male high school students if they would be afraid if a woman attacked them physically, the response is usually laughter. The question asked in reverse evokes a very different response. Even when physical assault does not occur or is rare, the type of intimidation and abuse described in this book is more characteristic of men than of women. Because of this, I refer to the *abuser* or *perpetrator* as "he" throughout.

At the same time I want to clearly acknowledge that men who are victims of abuse by women are in the same need of support and services as women (and may have greater difficulty in finding them), and that abuse occurs in same-sex couples as well as heterosexual couples. Research to date indicates domestic abuse occurs in gay and lesbian couples at approximately the same rate as heterosexual couples. Abuse occurs in married and unmarried romantic relationships and may emerge fairly quickly in a dating relationship.

Victim is an unsatisfactory term for a person who is the target of abuse because it connotes helplessness and defines a person in terms of the abuse. Defining oneself as a victim can contribute to a decision to tolerate abuse that should not be borne. *Survivor,* which is more respectful of the strength and resilience exhibited by women in these situations, also has limitations. Not all women do survive, physically or emotionally. More accurate and respectful terms would be "men who engage in abusive behavior" and "women who are the targets of abuse," but for the sake of brevity, I will use the terms *abuser, victim,* and *survivor* throughout.

Family abuse may be committed against children, partners, or elders. *Domestic abuse* is generally understood to mean abuse of intimate partners. The term *partner* includes married, unmarried, and formerly married abusers and victims.

One obstacle to identifying domestic abuse is that the terms *abuse* and *violence* are often used interchangeably. When people hear either term they picture all-out physical assault, a man seemingly out of control, destroying a home, and battering a woman senseless. Thousands of women endure such horrific violence every day, and their suffering should never be minimized. However, domestic abuse and violence are expressed through a range of behaviors, *all* of which have a powerful impact.

Violence indicates any physical or sexual assault of a person. It includes pushing or restraining another as well as punching, slapping, kicking, or using a weapon. Violence toward pets or inanimate objects can also be used as a means of intimidating a victim. Sometimes men use physical violence in the beginning of the relationship to establish a threatening atmosphere and don't see a need for violence later. Many men naturally become less physically violent as they age, though they rarely become less domineering without clear recovery work. In many cases violence escalates over time and becomes increasingly dangerous. Women gradually become accustomed to higher and higher levels of assault, and some eventually pay with their lives.

The term *abuse* means any behavior that is used to control, frighten, or humiliate another. In addition to physical and sexual violence and intimidation, abuse can be verbal, emotional, sexual, or financial. While physical assault can have legal consequences and is measurable to outsiders who are willing to acknowledge its presence, *emotional abuse* is much more confusing. Emotional abuse occurs when words, actions, and body language are used systematically to hurt and control another person. Physical or sexual abuse is always backed by emotional abuse. While everyone can be abusive at some times, partner abuse refers to a *systematic pattern* of abusive behavior intended to control another and inflict punishment on her.

Anger addiction is a term some people use when anger and abusive behavior become a primary coping mechanism to respond to pain and dissatisfaction. Like other types of addictive behavior, it is characterized by denial, compulsiveness, and distorted thought processes. Another name might be *abusive anger syndrome*. A syndrome is a predictable pattern of actions or symptoms. The *New Merriam-Webster Dictionary* defines a syndrome as "a group of signs or symptoms that occur together and characterize a particular abnormality." Abusers are strikingly similar in their motivations, thought processes, and goals, even when there is significant variation in their behavior.

Part One

Coming to Terms With Your Situation

These first three chapters focus on helping you understand the dynamics of abuse, making a decision to leave, and coping with stalking and harassment. These are grim realities, and the tone of these chapters reflects that. Much, but not all, of the attention is on understanding the abuser and his behavior.

Chapter 1 describes some of the causes of domestic abuse and the intentions underlying an abuser's choices. It speaks briefly to a victim's role in the complicated dance of abuse. It outlines characteristic markers of abuse: qualities found in many abusive relationships which can help you distinguish a pattern of abuse from the normal ups and downs of a challenging relationship.

Chapter 2 answers the hard question of why women stay in abusive relationships. This section describes the complex and painful process of deciding to leave and provides recommendations for those of you who want to support someone in an abusive relationship. There are guidelines for you to follow to determine whether an abuser is in fact changing and a reminder for abused women to take proper precautions before leaving.

Chapter 3 takes a sobering look at stalking and harassment. This section outlines reasons why abusers harass their partners and acknowledges the enormous power of harassment. It describes obvious and covert strategies abusers use to try to hold onto and punish their partners.

You can discover the truth of any situation by recognizing patterns. Movies, newspaper articles, and books about domestic abuse usually portray dramatic physical violence. In many abusive marriages physical violence is rare; words, money, sexual interactions, and humiliation are the weapons of choice. Harassment after separation may be covert, invisible to most people while being utterly oppressive to the woman targeted. The dynamics prompting all of this behavior are fundamentally the same: power, control, and punishment. Your freedom lies in recognizing the patterns of behavior and the motives that prompt them and then developing effective ways to protect yourself, tailored to your unique situation.

1

Understanding Partner Abuse

WHAT CAUSES DOMESTIC ABUSE?

Domestic abuse is confusing. Abuse is confusing in part because it seems to go against common sense and what is instinctively believed to be true about human behavior. When abuse happens to women, they are often stunned and bewildered. They are not alone in their confusion; professionals working in the field still struggle to understand abuse. Treatment programs for domestic abuse began just twenty-five years ago, and therapists and shelter staff still debate philosophy and strategies. What causes domestic abuse? What does it really look like? How can abusers and their partners be helped?

This debate is critically important. Witnessing or becoming the target of abuse can be paralyzing. Understanding can help abusers, survivors, their children, and the community break the spell and move toward freedom.

SEXISM AS A CAUSE OF DOMESTIC ABUSE

The Duluth Domestic Abuse Intervention Project is a national pioneer in the treatment of partner abuse. Michael Paymar, the former training coordinator for the project, has written two books, *Violent No More* and *Power and Control: The Tactics of Men Who Batter* (coauthored with Ellen Pence). The models in these books are used across the country. Paymar places primary emphasis on sexist attitudes and institutions in explaining abuse.

Seen from this perspective, domestic abuse is part of a pattern of *culturally approved violence against women.*

Throughout most of history, violence by men toward women has been considered an acceptable means of control and "discipline." In the past, incidents of extreme violence against women were reported to the Society for the Prevention of Cruelty to Animals.

In *Violent No More*, Paymar describes a telling incident he encountered while traveling. Delayed by some road construction, he stopped at the side of a highway and struck up a conversation with a stranger. The huge, tattooed man inquired about Paymar's line of work, and upon hearing the answer, offered this bit of wisdom.

> *"You wanna know why women get beat?" He seemed so confident.*
> *"Why?" I asked.*
> *He said, "I'll tell you why women get beat. They get beat 'cause they don't listen." And then he spit.*

Paymar expands:

> *When I think about the hundreds of men I've worked with over the years, except for the incidents of true self-defense, men batter (1) to get their partners to stop doing something they disapprove of, (2) to stop their partners from saying things or to end an argument, (3) to punish their partners for something they've done. It really is that simple.*[4]

While oppression of women is blatant in many countries, theoretically it is no longer accepted in the United States. Yet clear discrimination against women is in the very recent past, and core attitudes change slowly. Eighty years ago women were not allowed to vote. Just thirty years ago college women majored in education, nursing, and social work so they would have something to "fall back on" in case the men in their lives disappeared; few other career choices were available to them.

These lingering attitudes give silent approval to men who feel entitled to use physical force as a means of maintaining their dominance. I believe that sluggish responses on the part of police and the legal system stem largely from a belief that intimate violence against women is not as serious as assault by a stranger. These attitudes result from sexist beliefs and an exaggerated separation between public and private behavior.

Although sexist attitudes are changing, progress is uneven. Sexism is less overt in mainstream American culture and among those with higher levels of education. However, women still earn just 75 percent of men's income, and divorce or desertion leaves vast numbers of women caring for children in poverty or under very difficult conditions.

While women enjoy many new freedoms in education and employment, their private lives have not necessarily kept pace. Women do not enjoy equal benefits in America. Many homes at all educational and income levels are marred by abuse stemming from an expectation that men are entitled to power and control. In settings where violence against women is considered unacceptable, many men find other strategies to maintain the dominance they still believe is rightfully theirs. Immigrant women are among the most vulnerable members of society.

A truism in the field says, "Men abuse because they can." There seems to be a human tendency to want power and to use it disrespectfully when it is given in abundance. A significant number of men will continue to seriously abuse their partners as long as they are allowed to do so without consequences, and sexism sends a message to all men that they have permission to use their power destructively against women.

POOR ANGER MANAGEMENT SKILLS AS A CAUSE OF DOMESTIC ABUSE

If I ask my high school students what should be done with those who commit domestic abuse, someone is certain to pipe up and suggest anger management classes. It is true that domestic abuse is sometimes a result of *poor anger management skills*. Some people have simply not learned effective methods of handling anger and resort to violence because they do not know other ways to express their emotions. When this is the cause of abuse, men are generally willing to learn new skills and make changes in their behavior if offered the opportunity.

In cases of severe violence or abuse that occurs over an extended period of time, lack of skills is not likely to be the primary cause. In these cases, sending an abuser to anger management classes is roughly equivalent to signing up an alcoholic for a health class. The problem is not skills but motivation. Most abusers do not benefit from anger management classes because they have no desire to change their behavior.

SOCIALIZATION OF MALES AS A CAUSE OF DOMESTIC ABUSE

The manner in which families and societies train boys to become men is a significant cause of domestic and child abuse. Boys are taught at a very young age to hide their sadness and pain and to respond to stress without showing emotion. When I ask my male high school students at what age they learned not to cry, the answers range from eight down to three or four years old. Boys are taught to ignore their pain on the football field and in their relationships. Without a direct outlet for these powerful emotions, many men respond instead with anger. Anger is a valuable emotion, but when misdirected its value can be lost.

Anger is rarely the first emotion people feel even though it may be the first emotion to enter their awareness. When people get angry, they first had an experience that caused them to feel hurt, rejected, humiliated, sad, lonely, helpless, or another more vulnerable emotion. They become angry in order to protect themselves from those emotions and blunt the pain and helplessness.

Many people, particularly men, have difficulty identifying and expressing these underlying emotions. Women seem to be, or are socialized to be, more aware of these feelings and more expressive of them—they cry, talk to friends, or let them be known in other ways. Many men have been systematically taught not even to *acknowledge* feelings that carry vulnerability. From a young age they learn to suck it up, do without, carry on, tough it out, and not ask for help.

Over time many boys and men filter out much of the awareness that would help them be fully present to themselves and to a relationship. But those feelings do not go away. Without an outlet, they accumulate—and turn into anger. Over time these boys and men move toward anger more and more quickly, eventually becoming almost unaware that they are experiencing anything else. They learn to rely on anger to get what they want—or at least to express their displeasure at not having it. Part of the process of recovery for men is reconnecting with their vulnerability and learning to express it more productively.

While men have more permission now than in the past to be sensitive, they are still under strong pressure to hide their feelings. Often society—and women—give men confusing double messages. Women may say that they prefer men who can cry—but then react in distaste if they do. Often there is a very narrow margin of behavior that is considered acceptable for men. It should come as no surprise that many opt for the apparently safer path of avoiding intimate expression of emotion.

ADDICTIVE THOUGHT PROCESSES AND BEHAVIOR AS A CAUSE OF DOMESTIC ABUSE

While the role of sexist attitudes cannot be underestimated as a context for abuse, what often underlies a pattern of emotional or physical abuse is a *compulsive attachment to anger, abuse, and/or violence*. People who regularly engage in abusive behavior—which may or may not include physical violence—generally have thought processes and behaviors found in other addictive processes.

Because for so many years I did not name my experience as domestic abuse, I used what I knew about alcoholism and codependency to make some sense of what was happening in my family. As I continue to try to understand abuse, this comparison sheds further light on my life. The connection is also useful in helping other people understand abuse. Behavior that seems random or senseless can be understood quite readily when people apply what they know about other addictive processes.

Addictions arise as a response to pain and disappointment. People who are wounded in life—and in some way everyone has been— try to relieve their pain by engaging in some type of behavior. Some of those choices are helpful, like getting a hug, talking things over, taking a nap, or changing their circumstances. Other responses are negative, such as drinking alcohol excessively, arguing incessantly, driving recklessly, or clinging to relationships that aren't working.

Because negative behavior does not have the power to deal with the root cause of the pain, the suffering continues. Rather than finding another, more effective means of coping, some people simply repeat their actions more and more frequently. Alcoholics Anonymous calls this pattern insanity: doing the same thing over and over and expecting different results. With time, this behavior becomes increasingly habitual and unconscious.

In addition to responding to pain, addictions are an attempt to substitute people, substances, or behavior for more profound needs in a person's life, such as a sense of meaning and a relationship with a greater Power. Everyone makes these substitutions to some extent; some people do it more intensely and more destructively than others. People who move into full-blown addictions put less and less energy into finding helpful ways of managing their life, and their perceptions become progressively more distorted by denial. Eventually a person's direct control over his behavior is reduced, although it never disappears entirely.

The most significant predictor of becoming an abuser is to have experienced or witnessed abuse as a child. Childhood abuse, whether witnessed or experienced directly, leaves a huge reservoir of pain. Striking out is a natural, instinctive response to pain—most people have occasionally reacted angrily when they unexpectedly hit their head or stubbed their toe. Abusers develop a pattern of coping with pain and disappointment by striking out at those most vulnerable—their partners and, often, their children.

Recognizing the similarities between alcoholism and abuse can help people understand what they are seeing more quickly. Many people have a good basic understanding of alcoholism and realize that alcoholics engage in apparently irrational, highly damaging behavior. Although it is not a physical addiction, chronic abuse is like alcoholism in its compulsive nature, its origins, and the thought distortions that accompany it. The adrenaline rush that accompanies rage impacts the brain as directly as does alcohol. However, many domestic abuse treatment programs resist making this comparison.

The next few paragraphs may seem like an academic debate. However, they deal with a central question: the level of choice exerted by abusers. The answer to this question is critically important both to abusers and those who love them.

Most treatment programs do not speak of abuse as an addiction because of something called the "disease model." Alcoholics Anonymous and Al-Anon both describe alcoholism as a disease, and often base love and acceptance of the alcoholic on this perception. Members may say, when speaking of an alcoholic's outrageous behavior, "That's the disease talking, not the person; so why be angry at the person?" Statements such as these can be understood to let addicts off the hook for responsibility for their choices.

Domestic abuse programs strongly emphasize the *conscious choices* exercised by abusers, both in the interests of the abusers' recovery and the safety of their partners. Abusers will appear to be out of control when enraged, and perhaps they will claim this "loss of control" as an excuse. They will say, "I just lost it," "I couldn't help it," or "She made me do it." Yet they carefully choose who and when they will abuse, and the vast majority of abusers avoid taking on opponents who are able to respond in kind. Many are extremely sophisticated in their ability to hide their actions from outsiders and avoid consequences for themselves. The planning and deliberation involved in harassment are chilling evidence against the excuse that abusers unthinkingly act in the heat of the moment and are unable to control their behavior. Unlike chemical dependency, domestic abuse has not been labeled a mental illness by the American Medical Association.

An Al-Anon member once compared alcoholism to diabetes. People do not choose to have diabetes, but they do choose how to manage it. Alcoholics do not choose to be chemically dependent, but they do choose whether or not to enter a recovery program. Abusers did not choose to grow up in a sexist culture or to be abused as children, but they determine how they will respond. Once a pattern of abuse has been established it is extremely difficult to break, just as it is extremely difficult for an alcoholic to refrain from taking a second drink. Diabetics, alcoholics, and abusers all exercise their freedom in deciding whether or not to engage in a program that will help them effectively manage their condition. Neither alcoholics nor abusers come to that decision until *they* decide their behavior is no longer working for them—an indication that a significant, if not wholly conscious, level of choice is operating. Like alcoholics, few abusers are able to significantly alter their life without professional help and a consistent program of recovery.

I do not believe there is a disease that takes over an abuser and separates him from the good person God created. Over time, denial has clouded his perceptions, and his freedom to choose has been limited by the habitual nature of his response to stress. But he is capable of choosing to reverse that process and to deal with his pain and anger in a more constructive way.

Choice is at the heart of recovery. Very few alcoholics are able to move toward health on their own, barring a profound spiritual experience. Yet those who *do* recover recall a moment in time when they made a fundamental shift in desire. At some point they decided they'd had enough, that it was time to stop what they were doing. That process remains something of a mystery, unique to each person. People who have been there describe a paradoxical reality, where a new awareness of their own choices and the limitations of human will power intersect. For many, this is a time of discovering that only God has the necessary power to bring about deep change. While recovery takes time, hard work, and outside help, it begins with a fundamental decision to live life differently. In order to recover, abusers must come to a similar decision.

THE GOALS OF ABUSE

So often an abused woman finds herself asking, "Why did he do that?" Even apparently irrational behavior is purposeful. To understand an abuser's behavior a woman needs to discover the purpose behind the choices. She needs to understand her abuser's intentions in order to be able to strategize effectively to protect herself. By way of comparison, until society understood that rape was a crime of power rather than of sexual desire, it could not begin to solve the issue. Until families grasp that anorexia is about control rather than food, all their efforts to help will be misdirected.

Many domestic abuse treatment programs assume that the goals of abuse are power and control. Certainly the goals of sexism are power and control. However, the goal of those hooked on anger and abuse is also vengeance: to punish another for the pain, stress, and disappointment abusers experience in their own lives.

Many women attempt to fulfill a partner's every wish in order to escape punishment, but even a completely compliant partner cannot avoid pain. An abusive man will drag a sleeping woman out of bed and beat her simply because he has had a bad day. The adrenaline rush that accompanies the expression of rage is a "high," and abusers become hooked on the temporary sense of power and release that follows. The pure vindictiveness and excessive cruelty of abusers' behavior cannot be explained as simply a means of gaining power and control; satisfaction in the ability to inflict pain and humiliation on another person is a recurring element of abuse. In addition, some men crave the false intimacy and self-pity that frequently follow the abuse.

All human beings are complex, and abusers are no exception. Some men use power and control primarily in order to keep a woman in range of punishment; others use punishment as a means of exerting power and control.

Whatever the mix, it is important to acknowledge and accept the clear intention to harm that underscores abuse.

ABOUT CODEPENDENCY

While understanding the abuser is important, a primary focus of this book is to help women reclaim their lives and souls after being in an abusive relationship. Just as abusers share some common characteristics, women who are in abusive relationships also tend to behave in some predictable ways. My first insight into my own choices came many years ago when I first heard the term "codependency."

Approximately thirty years ago, professionals working with alcoholics noticed certain predictable patterns of behavior in the alcoholic's spouse and children. Over time, these patterns of coping, established as a response to a loved one's alcoholism, became known as codependency. Some characteristics of codependency are an unwillingness to care for oneself in a healthy way and a preoccupation with attempting to take care of and control the destructive behavior of others. One definition of codependence is "caring about other people's lives more than they do."

Women trying to survive in an abusive relationship exhibit similar characteristics. Some learned these patterns in their families of origin and then reinforced them in their partner relationship.

Others developed them in an attempt to survive and maintain some sense of balance while living with an abuser. Women progressively become more and more focused on trying to manage their partners' behavior—to pacify, to placate, to persuade, to somehow control the abuse in order to find safety for themselves and their children.

Like abuse, codependency also shares some of the characteristics of an addiction. It is an unproductive pattern of response to a painful situation or a lack of love or meaning in life. The following table includes a comparison of codependency and abuse with other more widely recognized addictive patterns. The core dynamic is the same, although the victim's behavior and thought processes exhibit some differences.

	CHEMICAL DEPENDENCY	EATING DISORDER	ANGER ADDICTION	CODEPENDENCE
Goals of Behavior	Avoid pain and responsibility by altering mood with chemicals	Gain sense of safety and control by reducing weight	Avoid responsibility and discharge pain by inflicting punishment on another	Seek safety and avoid dealing with own life by caretaking others
Primary Bearer(s) of Consequences	Self, with blatant disregard for others	Self	Target(s) of abuse	Self, with others as secondary victims
Distorted Self-Perception	See self as victim	See self as "fat" and powerless	See self as victim	See self as rescuer
Compulsive Behavior	Getting drunk or high	Restricting food intake, exercising, bingeing/purging	Frightening, humiliating, and hurting others physically, sexually, or emotionally	Taking action to "positively" manage others' behavior, thoughts, and emotions
Denial	Dependence on chemicals, impact of behavior on self and others	Negative impact of behavior on health	Intention to abuse, ability to control behavior and extent of harmful impact on others	Others' right to autonomy, codependent's own needs and limitations

An essential element in recovering from codependency is moving the focus of attention from the abuser to the woman's life. This is riskier and more complex than learning to let go of a loved one that is alcoholic or anorexic. Chapters 3 and 4 outline the challenges and risks of learning to step out of the dance with an abusive partner. It is a difficult process, but it is an essential part of reclaiming your freedom.

CHARACTERISTIC MARKERS OF DOMESTIC ABUSE

Partner abuse has characteristic "markers" that, when understood, are fairly easy to recognize, just as people who are familiar with alcoholism or eating disorders can quickly recognize symptoms in a client or loved one. Victims of domestic abuse are no more to blame for their partners' behavior than are spouses of alcoholics. They can find lasting help only from therapists who recognize the signs of abuse and are able to separate them from the normal flawed relationship patterns that are the stuff of life.

Couples, marriage counselors, churches, family, and friends often view domestic abuse as a marriage problem. This misperception causes unnecessary misery for couples, because the symptoms of abuse go unrecognized and the victim may be blamed for the abuse or made more vulnerable to it. Those who commit abuse are responsible for their actions.

THE CYCLE OF ABUSE

Lenore Walker's classic work, *The Battered Woman,* identifies a distinctive, predictable cycle of abuse that appears in approximately two-thirds of all cases.[5] This cycle can repeat itself hundreds of times during a relationship. The stages of the cycle are not simply sequential, but through the distorted logic of the abuser, each stage *produces* the next step.

Stage One: The Honeymoon Phase. Many abusers go through periods where they are kind, thoughtful, and charming. The early stages of a relationship often exhibit only this phase of the cycle. In fact, a warning sign that a relationship may turn abusive is if a man is *too* attentive and infatuated with a woman upon meeting her. It is the hope for a return to this idyllic phase that seduces many women into staying in abusive relationships well beyond the point of reason.

Therapist and author David Decker's treatment model renames this the deception phase.[6] The abuser's intention is to deceive the victim, and to some degree himself, into thinking the abuse is an aberration. The abuser presents himself as warm, attentive, and loving. The effort required to maintain this deception causes him to build up resentment, which then moves the cycle into its second stage.

Stage Two: Tension. During this period the abuser experiences stress and growing irritability. After convincing himself during stage one that he is a wonderful partner, he increasingly interprets events as justifying his more fundamental perception of himself as a victim. Outside stresses can also contribute to the tension buildup. During this stage the abuser may become cold and distant or engage in smaller incidents of abuse that increase in frequency and severity.

Stage Three: The Crisis. During this phase abusers discharge the tension accumulated during the previous stages. They cut loose with physical and/or sexual assault, or extreme verbal or emotional abuse. They experience a sense of power and release while enraged and may feel relaxed and even euphoric afterward.

Abusers may feel contrite after an incident, although this remorse generally lessens over time as the pattern becomes more established. Abusers then move back into the deception phase in order to reconcile with the victim and to ensure that she stays within range for the next episode. As this cycle becomes established, the first and second phases typically become shorter and often disappear altogether. The cycle may disappear and reappear over the course of an extended relationship.

DENIAL

Denial is a refusal to recognize reality. In culturally accepted violence against women, abusers deny the essential dignity and equality of women. In some cultures this denial is so thoroughly reinforced that even healthy and responsible men and women accept it as truth.

Denial is also a hallmark of addiction, and abusers who have an addictive pattern of anger demonstrate a level of denial that is perplexing to victims and outsiders. This denial takes three forms:

1. Denial of the behavior. Abusers will deny that an incident took place or minimize its severity. Some abusers are capable of breaking a partner's arm and then innocently asking her what happened.

2. Denial of the consequences. Some abusers will acknowledge their actions but deny that they have frightened, hurt, or humiliated the victim. They also vehemently deny that the abuser himself should experience any consequences as a result of his actions.

3. Denial of responsibility. Even the most violent abusers invariably see themselves as victims. They feel powerless and justify their actions by saying the victim made them do it, deserved the abuse, or that they were incapable of stopping themselves.[7]

Many abusers will go to great lengths to hide their behavior from outsiders in order to keep the denial intact. It is common for abusers to leave physical marks and bruises only on those parts of their victims' bodies that will not be seen in public. After separation, many men develop elaborate and successful strategies to deceive friends and family members about the cause of their breakup. A primary goal of treatment programs is to help abusers break through their denial and develop empathy for their victims. Abusers fight desperately to maintain their denial because it protects their perceived right to continue to abuse.

"JEKYLL AND HYDE PERSONALITY"

Treatment programs often use the term "Jekyll and Hyde Personality" to describe their clients. Abuse is confusing because so many abusers have wide variations in their behavior. Most are not consistently abusive with their partners, children, or outsiders. Incidents of abuse are particularly shattering because victims are taken by surprise at their partners' lightning-quick mood changes, making any moment unpredictable.

Abusers are often appealing and affable with outsiders, and many never inflict their anger on anyone other than their partners or children. Some men abuse only their partners, others only their children. Many alternate, keeping family dynamics in a constant state of turmoil.

The abuser's ability to charm outsiders makes it difficult for his victim to speak up and receive support, because the contrast between his public and private actions is so great. Outsiders have great difficulty believing that someone who appears so warm, relaxed, and engaging could possibly commit serious abuse. Some abusers are shy in public, lacking the self-confidence to be assertive with others. Outsiders may find it unbelievable that such a self-effacing person could be dangerously aggressive. This contrast contributes to the victim's sense of disbelief and her difficulty in taking action to protect herself.

DEPRIVATION AND ENTITLEMENT

Abusers see themselves as victims, which grants them a sense of entitlement. They feel deprived, either by past experiences of abuse, disappointment, or loss or by an event in the present moment. When men act out of sexist attitudes, they feel deprived of their "legitimate" privileges when a woman does not cater to their desires or questions their authority. As a result of this deprivation, abusers feel entitled to compensation. They believe a partner owes them unswerving devotion and compliance. Compensation takes the form of a license to control, to inflict pain, and to cross boundaries. For men this sense of entitlement is often culturally reinforced. Abusers feel entitled to inflict suffering because of the pain they have experienced themselves. The longer an abusive relationship lasts, the more entrenched this attitude becomes. A sense of entitlement gives abusers internal permission to inflict enormous harm on their partners and children while feeling little, if any, guilt or remorse.

2

Discovering When and How to Leave

No woman is foolish enough to stay with a man who beats her up on the first date. Every human being has good in him or her, and women who become involved with abusive men respond to something attractive they see at the beginning. Many abusers court a woman in the early stages of a relationship, showering her with attention. In other cases, women are attracted to what they see as tenderness and vulnerability masked under a tough guy exterior.

Some abusers reveal their true nature during courtship, and women may walk away as the darker side emerges. But many abusers are exceptionally aware of the power they wield and do not take off the mask until they feel secure in their position. "Melanie" was advised to relocate thousands of miles away from her home because her husband was so dangerous. The counselor asked her when she discovered her husband's true nature, and Melanie replied that he first brutally beat her on their wedding night. Her story is not unique.

Some men become abusive when pregnancy or childbirth shifts the balance of power or distracts a woman from devoting herself entirely to him. The longer a relationship lasts and the greater her investment, the more difficulty a woman has in leaving. This chapter will look at why women stay in abusive relationships, how they transition toward a decision to leave, and how to find proper resources to sustain and protect them as they go.

IN THE BEGINNING

Many new relationships begin hopefully. A woman meets someone and finds him attractive; her expectations rise as she invites this new person into her life. Emotions can be especially strong when the new person is a potential life partner. Most people yearn for someone special to share life's ongoing challenges and joys. Particularly in today's mobile and fragmented society, life as a single person can be lonely. A woman wants to be able to love someone, to give herself to someone who will be there tomorrow and the next day. Men and women naturally search for someone who will reassure them when they're uncertain, love them when they fail, know who they really are, and stay with them anyway.

Of course, people are imperfect. They disappoint each other every day. Humans are limited, and no one can supply *all* the affirmation and companionship a person needs. People are less appealing when they roll out of bed in the morning, when they get grouchy, when they disagree with each other. Accepting the limitations of relationships is part of becoming an adult.

People should evaluate their relationships on an ongoing basis. Some relationships belong in a woman's life, in spite of their limitations. Others need to be let go. Ending a relationship is often painful, whether it be a friendship or a romantic relationship. The hurt may come progressively, in isolated moments when a woman recognizes the person she is with is not the person she imagined. The pain may come in a rush at the end, when the other person bids her good-bye or she finally allows herself to see what her inner wisdom, family, and friends have been telling her all along. When a relationship ends it is natural to want to resist pain and to avoid seeing it when it is present.

There is always a gap between a person's best behavior and worst behavior. Most people are on their best behavior in the beginning of a relationship—particularly with a potential mate—and have their worst moments with people they interact with on a daily basis. For just this reason, family has been called the place where, when you have to go there, they have to take you in. In healthy people, the gap between best and worst behavior is limited.

With many abusers, the distance between first impressions and long-term reality is not a gap—it is a chasm. The true character of an abuser may bear no resemblance at all to the man who first shows up at her door.

WHY WOMEN STAY

The classic response to hearing about an abusive relationship is, "But why does she stay?" People think, "*I* would never put up with that. *I* would have walked out the first time he did that to me." Women stay in abusive relationships for a variety of reasons; few situations are as simple as they appear. Women struggling to end a relationship need to be affirmed in the complexity of their dilemma. Paradoxically, clarity and reassurance about her decision to *stay* helps bring about the strength and self-esteem necessary to *leave*. Professionals, family, and friends of an abused woman can dramatically improve their support by understanding her decision to stay in a relationship. Judgmental comments and lack of empathy from others make her reluctant to speak up, and an isolated woman has greater difficulty leaving. Victims stay for the following reasons:

- Because of the good times
- Redeeming their investment
- Fear of retaliation
- Protecting their children
- Fear of being alone
- Economics
- Love

- Confusion
- Religion
- Bad advice

BECAUSE OF THE GOOD TIMES

"There is some good in the worst of us and some bad in the best of us." This old saying carries a great deal of wisdom. It also expresses the confusion of women caught in abusive relationships. All abusers have good qualities, although over the course of time those good qualities may be largely buried. Few men are abusive all the time, and fewer still are consistently abusive at the beginning of a relationship.

In the beginning, many abusers are wonderful partners. They may write love notes and send flowers, tell a woman how attractive she is and how important she is in his life. He may be protective of her, jealous, wary of other men, seeming to value his partner so much he can't stand being away from her.

Sometimes the good times exist largely in a woman's imagination. Some women hope so desperately to find a man who will love them that they attach that dream to someone who clearly does not have good intentions. Whether the good times are real, imagined, or simply misunderstood, they are powerful. The experiences begin the process of binding a woman to the relationship, storing up memories that tie her to her partner. At some point, the dream starts to fray as abuse enters the picture. But the early days, or the early dreams, are a vivid memory, one the victim naturally clings to.

Human beings respond to conditioning. Psychologists speak of classical conditioning, which works on animals as well as humans. For example, in the morning when my dogs hear me turn off the security system and unlock the front door, they get restless, because they anticipate that I will be letting them out soon. Their brains have stored the information that the sound of doors unlocking at that time of day means freedom for them.

Intermittent gratification is one of the more powerful forms of learning. Intermittent gratification occurs when good things happen irregularly or unexpectedly. Because a woman has limited control over the outcome and is not sure when it will happen, she invests more in trying to create that result, particularly if the outcome is important to her.

Gambling packs a wallop because it delivers results intermittently. Gamblers can lose vast amounts of money in an evening and win it back before the end of the night. The outcome is unpredictable, and a gambler never knows when his increased risk-taking will pay off. Women in abusive relationships become relationship gamblers. The exciting, warm, wonderful moments are the prize.

Just as abuse is intermittent in many relationships, the honeymoon period appears unexpectedly as well. Abusers often have an uncanny ability to tell when a woman has reached her limit and will then shift gears to woo her back. To a disinterested bystander, the manipulation may be obvious. But the desire on her part to return to the loving moments, despite the unpredictability of their appearance, can be hard to resist.

For women who grew up in abusive or neglectful families, honeymoon times with an abuser may be the only moments of attention and security they have known. The desire to return to those moments, and to cling to the belief that they are real and the abuse is an accident or unintentional, can be very strong.

The contrast between the "good" and "bad" behavior exhibited by many abusers contributes to the tension. The discrepancy is so enormous it is almost unbelievable. Journalist Michelle Weldon tells of her experiences with her abuser's contrasting behaviors in the book *I Closed My Eyes*. Her husband, a successful attorney and former college boxer, would give her one powerful, debilitating punch when he wanted to settle an argument. Yet he continued to write love notes to her throughout their relationship. Weldon included excerpts of these notes in her book, such as the one below, written late in their marriage, when the violence had escalated to a dangerous level.

> *Dearest Michelle . . .*
>
> *I know it is a difficult time for you. You fight rejection continually for work that you know is beyond compare. Well, I can only say that I believe in you and I pray for you constantly. You will succeed. Your dreams will come true. Just stay attuned to the abilities God has given you. They will come to fruition. I also know what a tremendous mother you are. . . . I realize that you feel like an alien with all of these boys around the house. All I can say is that we love you and we won't lose sight of what you mean to us.*[8]

Most women would be thrilled to receive such a sensitive and loving letter. It is hard to understand how those sentiments can coexist with violence and a desire to kill. A woman naturally wants to believe the best of those she loves, and a spiritual approach to life calls her to be compassionate and forgiving on principle. To anyone who does not have the desire to hurt others deliberately and without reason, abuse is incomprehensible. It is as if a chair suddenly turned into a cougar and then a few hours later turned back into a chair. The experience is so out of the realm of possibility that people tend to tell themselves it couldn't have happened.

For many women, abuse is so foreign to their ethical view of the world and to their experience outside of the home that, in spite of repeated experiences to the contrary, it remains unbelievable. It is not just hard to understand *why* abuse happens, it is difficult to truly comprehend *that* it happens. This is particularly true with men who seem kind and caring most of the time.

Humans seem to have a limited ability to retain contradictory information, at least on an emotional level. Extreme seasonal changes provide a comparison. In Minnesota when it is 95 degrees outside with 80 percent humidity, I cannot remember what it feels like to be cold, although I know with dead certainty that I will be chilled to the bone the following winter. Six months later, on a day with a –50-degree windchill, I cannot register the sensation of sweltering in the heat.

Variability in weather does not carry the emotional kick of variability in relationships. Because the extremes of an abusive relationship are so intimate and so close to a woman's desire for emotional survival, they are very difficult to leave behind. Memories of the good times, a desire to return to them, and an inability to comprehend that those moments are not authentic, all hold women in relationships that are not good for them.

REDEEMING THEIR INVESTMENT

Women constantly invest in enterprises, whether they be a relationship, the stock market, or a job. They assess the risks and benefits and decide to commit some of their hopes, prospects, money, or time. Investments are always uncertain, and women can only discover *after* they commit if the investment was worthwhile.

When difficulties arise, a woman will stop and evaluate. If she quit every undertaking when it became difficult or unpleasant, she would never accomplish anything. However, if she stays too long with a losing proposition, she only increases her losses. I remember hearing a radio program on America's decision to increase its involvement in Vietnam. According to the commentator, once a significant number of young lives had been lost, people felt a need to win the war in order to make those tragic deaths worthwhile. As casualties continued to rise, the need intensified to redeem them by bringing about a positive resolution to the conflict.

As a woman's losses mount in an abusive relationship, the desire can become more intense to make it work, to somehow redeem those painful times and make them worthwhile. As abuse increases and becomes more obvious, a woman can become perversely locked into the relationship, trying to somehow make it come out right. Unless the abuser chooses to move into recovery, however, this effort is doomed to failure. Chapters 7 and 8 deal in greater depth with grieving and letting go of losses, a critical component of finally becoming free.

FEAR OF RETALIATION

Abuse invariably escalates when a woman tries to leave a relationship. Ending a relationship threatens a man's control over his partner and causes him stress, which he vents by further punishing his partner. Studies show the most dangerous time for women is during separation and the first two years after divorce. Some men who have not been physically violent unexpectedly escalate to lethal violence during separation.

Many men hold on to a partner by threatening to harm her, their children, or himself if she leaves. Women know that partners who seem largely disinterested can become totally focused if they try to escape. Many women expect retaliation if they try to end a relationship. They are rarely surprised.

PROTECTING THEIR CHILDREN

The presence of children increases the complexity and unpredictability of leaving a relationship. Most terrifying is the potential for physical harm on the part of an enraged abuser. Some men have been known to kidnap their children and hold them hostage until a partner returns. A horrifying case occurred in Minnesota a number of years ago. A young man who was angry with his girlfriend took his revenge on their six-month-old son. Alone in the car with the child, the man head-butted the defenseless infant and then slammed his head against the dashboard. He finished by hurling the baby out of the car, killing him. Stories like these can be powerful deterrents to women thinking of leaving an abuser.

Some men will threaten to take custody of children away from their mothers. Contrary to what most people believe, men currently win approximately two-thirds of court cases where custody is contested. The possibility of losing her children is terrifying to a mother, particularly if the father is abusive. Even if a woman gains primary custody of her children, the prospect of an abusive partner being allowed unsupervised visitation can be enough to hold some women in a relationship. In many states, partner abuse is not considered when awarding custody and visitation rights, which leaves women and children vulnerable to the vindictiveness of a former partner.[9] While some women unwisely put their children at risk by staying in a relationship for selfish reasons, the threat to children when ending a relationship should never be underestimated.

Many women stay because they feel maintaining an intact family is best for their children. This is particularly true if the abuse does not include physical assault, or if the abuser assaults his partner but not his children. "Cindy's" decision to divorce was excruciating because she did not believe her children were better off apart from their father—as long as she was there to intervene when necessary. Her parents had divorced, and even though she agreed with their decision, she was profoundly saddened by the final disintegration of her family of origin, the people with whom she had shared the early years of her life. She knew she had to leave her husband in order to survive but felt as though her only escape was against the best interests of her children. She struggled for years before finally deciding to leave.

The enormity of the decision to break up a family is overwhelming. Women bear the terrible responsibility of making a decision that will forever alter not only their own lives but also those of the children they have been given to love and protect. Each child is unique, with different strengths, weaknesses, and relationships with his or her parents. At any given moment, divorce might be beneficial for one child and harmful for another.

Many men abandon their children after divorce. Women who expect this outcome from their partners can struggle with making a decision they know will cause their children pain. A conscientious mother's burden is profound.

Some children plead for the family to stay together, and initiating a divorce has the potential of estranging them from their mother. The strain on these relationships can be heartbreaking at a time when the victim is incurring other enormous losses. Even when a father is abusive or neglectful, children hunger for affirmation from him. This hunger can lead them to deny the reality of the abuse they witness and experience.

Children, however, are often wiser than adults realize. Many children want their parents to divorce and end the abuse and discord but do not have the words or the courage to broach the subject themselves. Their initial shock on hearing of divorce does not necessarily reflect their deepest feelings. When the students in my high school classes speak of their parents' divorce, many of them express relief that the conflict is over and family members are free to move on with their lives.

FEAR OF LONELINESS

Men and women do not enter a level playing field after divorce. Women still provide the majority of care for children, and being a single parent while holding down a job and running a household is exhausting. Single mothers often have a hard time maintaining friendships, let alone finding time or opportunity for dating. Divorce often fractures a couples' social circle, giving rise to the refrain, "Who gets custody of the friends?" While many men leave friendships behind, abusers who have a positive public image may take over a circle of friends and deliberately exclude their former wives, leaving them yet more isolated.

Men find new partners more readily for a variety of reasons.

- Men are often unencumbered or less encumbered by caring for children.

- Women are generally more willing to enter a relationship with a partner who has children than are men.

- The economic disadvantages of divorce weigh more heavily on women than on men, making women less desirable to a potential new partner.

- Society's norms allow older men to date younger women, while women are usually confined to a smaller pool of older men.

As women age, these disadvantages increase. It is no wonder women hesitate before embarking on such a lonely journey.

ECONOMICS

In spite of women's financial progress in recent years, economic factors still weigh heavily in a victim's decision to stay with her partner. Many women fear they may not be able to support themselves and their children. Many abusive men control the family finances, and women lack information about family assets or do not have access to them. Men may engage in hideously expensive legal battles around custody or assets.

Women who have been home with children for many years may lack the skills or current qualifications to reenter the job market at a reasonable level. Therefore, women earning relatively low wages can be crippled by the cost of childcare. In some cases the abuser cared for the children while the woman worked. Some fathers provide decent care for their children—care that is difficult to replace. Reliable childcare is scarce as well as expensive. Some men use a woman's difficulty in finding quality childcare against her in a custody battle.

Keeping a job as a single parent can be difficult. Single mothers sometimes are forced to miss work because of sick children. Many men harass their partners at work, causing some women to lose their jobs. The late Senator Paul Wellstone proposed federal legislation that would make it illegal for employers to fire women who are harassed in the workplace by former partners; the Victims' Economic Security and Safety Act has yet to be passed into law.

Approximately 50 percent of awarded child support is actually paid. It would be reasonable to assume that abusers have a higher-than-average level of nonpayment. It is therefore understandable that women weigh economics very carefully before deciding to leave.

LOVE

Many victims genuinely love their abusers. In addition to yearning for a return to the love they felt they received at the beginning of the relationship or that seems to recur at times in the relationship, women have an altruistic concern for their partners' welfare. They fear for his well-being if they leave, and some men's threats of suicide compound these fears. A woman may have compassion for the wounds she knows are at the root of her partner's abusive behavior and believes her love can somehow heal him and bring him back to wholeness. Women see the goodness and vulnerability these men often try to hide. The more kind and tenderhearted a woman is, the harder it may be for her to grasp the true nature of her partner's abuse and the level of hostility behind it. Unfortunately, once a pattern of abuse is established, consequences, rather than warmth, hold the greatest potential for change.

CONFUSION

An abuser is quick to remind his victim of her shortcomings. But the fact that she is angry or brings her own issues to a relationship is never an excuse or a cause for abuse. Awareness of her own negative contributions may confuse a woman about whether she has a right to leave. She does. While it is always important for a woman to take responsibility for her own behavior and work to better it, increased patience or compassion is highly unlikely to bring about a change in her abuser's behavior. The victim didn't cause the abuse, she can't control it, and she can't cure it. Abusers, like alcoholics, decide to change when they perceive their behavior no longer works *for them.*

RELIGION

Many faith traditions have strong teaching on the sacredness of marriage. Some women stay in abusive marriages out of a mistaken belief that God requires it. They may have asked for advice from clergy or other church professionals, perhaps without disclosing the full severity of the abuse. They may have been advised to go back, try harder, pray more, or try marriage counseling. Some women are told their suffering is their path to heaven.

Many couples go to clergy for counseling. While many religious leaders are wise in human relationships, most of them are not trained in psychology and are woefully uninformed on abuse. Women should not expect more help from them than they can be expected to give.

A victim needs to bear in mind that in addition to upholding marriage, most religious traditions also clearly defend the sacred dignity of the human person. I stayed in my marriage for twenty-four years because, as a Catholic, I took my marriage promises very seriously. I thought that unless my husband put me in the hospital or showed obvious signs of mental illness, I was required to stay and try to make it work. Abuse that is present from the beginning of a marriage, even if it does not include serious physical violence, is grounds for annulment within the Catholic Church. The annulment process, while unpleasant, was an important public statement for me that God does *not* require submission to abuse as a sign of faithfulness to his will.

Women who value their faith tradition should seek out wise counsel and not assume they are required to stay in a marriage that is destructive to the person God created them to be.

BAD ADVICE

Because the general public is so misinformed on domestic abuse, many women receive inappropriate feedback when they try to address the abuse in their relationship. As "Clare" was approaching her absolute emotional limit before ending her marriage, the counselor she was seeing at the time unwisely assigned her the task of becoming more vulnerable and less "parental" in her marriage. When she protested that this seemed foolhardy if her husband was not working on his anger, the counselor assured her he was confident that very soon her husband would begin that work. That faulty professional advice depleted emotional reserves she desperately needed for the difficult transition out of her marriage.

Many women drop hints to friends or family about what is happening in their homes. People often resist hearing them in an attempt to avoid disturbing family or community peace. If a man is abusive only in private, outsiders may have trouble believing what a woman says or will minimize its importance. If the abuse does not include physical assault, many well-meaning people ascribe it to marital problems and encourage her to look on the bright side. Advising women to be patient, forgive, get marriage counseling, and start over perpetuate the cycle and make it more difficult for victims to summon up the resolve to leave.

DECIDING TO LEAVE

Ending an abusive relationship can be remarkably difficult. The average survivor leaves her abuser seven times before making the final break.

Women who stay in abusive relationships progressively mangle their internal warning systems. Some women's alarm systems were seriously damaged before becoming involved with an abuser; others sustain new or further damage while with one. The reasonable response to abuse is to confront it, clearly request that it stop, and to get out of range if it continues. Women in abusive relationships cannot stop the abuse, but for a variety of reasons they have chosen not to get out of range. They have learned over thousands of interactions to override their instinct to flee. In trying to love and see the best in an abuser, victims teach themselves to ignore what they know to be true.

Coming to a decision to leave requires a woman to pay attention to the problems she ignored in the past and reconnect with her own wisdom. The longer the relationship has lasted, or the more it duplicates the victim's experience from her family of origin or other relationships, the harder it will be for her to reverse this conditioning. The decision to leave does not happen overnight, although women may be unconscious of their progress in that direction. The decision to leave generally comes as a result of:

- learning new information,
- reaching a limit of tolerance for the abuse,
- finding a moment of clarity,
- discerning God's will,
- assessing the likelihood of the abusers' recovery, and
- gathering the necessary resources to leave.

LEARNING NEW INFORMATION

Unfortunately, being a target of abuse does not necessarily make victims experts on the topic. In retrospect, I think I understood approximately 85 percent of the implications of my former husband's behavior. I knew by the end of our first year of marriage that he was abusive, that it came from his own background and choices and not from mine, and that he resisted making any permanent change. But there was a critical 15 percent I did not understand that kept me in the marriage.

"Kathryn" took a step toward leaving when she heard a domestic abuse counselor address a college class on women's issues. The speaker described the cycle of abuse and noted that police or professional intervention typically comes after an explosion, when the couple is beginning to move back into the honeymoon phase. The speaker noted that this is the least effective time for intervention, and Kathryn realized her futile attempts to bring about change occurred at exactly this stage of the cycle. The speaker's observation that men abuse "because they can" planted the seeds of awareness in Kathryn that gradually and unconsciously deepened over time. She left her abuser a year later.

Each piece of new information brings the abuser's behavior, and the victim's responses to it, into greater clarity. Because women have ignored their own inner wisdom so often and because the myths about domestic abuse are so powerful, it can take a lot of repetition for the truth to travel from their brain to their gut. They need to hear a principle and then see its accuracy demonstrated in real life. It may have taken hundreds or even thousands of repetitions for women to adjust themselves to abuse; it is not surprising that they require time and repetition to adjust themselves to a more healthy view of life. Few women can decide to leave before that deeper understanding takes hold. They may need to go through several cycles of abuse before a new insight is truly integrated into their awareness.

Attending a group for recovering women can be enormously helpful for those who are considering leaving as well as for those who have left. The clarity that comes with hearing others' stories and the shared strength in the presence of other survivors is very important. Women can hear each other speak and realize that at the core their stories are the same. The sheer repetition of hearing the lessons over and over helps them readjust their worldview to align more closely with reality. Survivors can understand each other's experiences in a way that no one else can.

My group leader, Laura, often reminded my recovery group that wherever a nonrecovering abuser is, he is always in his cycle. It is both sobering and enlightening to realize that no matter how kind or caring he might seem at the moment, a nonrecovering abuser will always, always, always return to abuse. Any new insight sheds light on a victim's experience and may eventually move her closer to the door.

REACHING A LIMIT OF TOLERANCE FOR THE ABUSE

Some women leave because the accumulation of abuse simply becomes too much. They recognize that the relationship has deteriorated. The abuse may have become worse, or their love for their partner has simply run out. Women may see the toll the abuse is taking on their children, both in the pain they experience and the unwise choices they begin to make in their own lives. The abuse may have escalated to the point where women realize there will be irreparable damage to themselves or their children if they stay. Many women wait until the last possible moment, when it seems they are on the point of no return, before finally giving themselves permission to leave an impossible situation.

MOMENTS OF CLARITY

Recovering alcoholics speak of moments of clarity when reality breaks through the clouds that obscure the truth. Often these moments are prompted by relatively trivial events that somehow strike a nerve and cause the alcoholic to take a hard look at where their choices have brought them. For example, an alcoholic who drank his way through thirty years of marriage chose sobriety when his son would no longer allow him to visit his grandchildren while drunk.

Whenever women are in a destructive situation, whether caused by their own or others' choices, they filter out some information as a means of survival. Actually, they filter out a lot of information. Women living with their abusers have become accustomed to frightening, demeaning, unpredictable eruptions as a matter of course. Events they would not have tolerated early in the relationship become a normal part of life. Yet it is never too late to see the truth.

Victims who are older made a decision to stay at a time when their understanding of abuse was more limited than it is today. If they had left when they "should" have, they would not have their children, a gift mothers would never give up. They would not have the wisdom and compassion they gained from their most difficult times.

Each situation is unique. If I had left my husband even a year earlier, I would not have found the professional resources I needed to truly recover. Women cannot know fully the costs and benefits resulting from their choices. So far, I have not regretted my decision to stay for so long. I have mourned the cost to me and my children, but I am at peace with my past.

An axiom of recovery programs and shelters is: "Every woman has her own time." Women will not leave before they are ready, although the process of getting to that decision may be agonizing.

"Davina" had a moment of clarity when her husband shoved their son into a wall, and she realized she no longer had the strength to protest. Clarity came to "Caroline" when her husband knocked her to the ground and her head hit the corner of a table, repeating an incident she had endured as a child at the hands of her mother. For Michelle Weldon, author of *I Closed My Eyes*, her decision came when she heard her husband whisper during an attack, "Please, God, let me kill her."

Moments of clarity are unique to each person. Final clarity arrived for me when my former husband began an abuse treatment program but did not do the assigned homework. A month later I recognized the beginning of the next abuse cycle. One evening I entered our front porch just as my former husband began another angry outburst. I have absolutely no recollection what he said.

What I know is that I heard the words, *It's time*, very clearly in my head. I knew that at last I was free to begin my journey out of the storm of abuse.

DISCERNING GOD'S WILL

For many women the decision to stay or leave is a spiritual process. Each step along the way, women pray for change, for healing, and for guidance, trying to discern what God is asking of them. They try to open themselves to God's light in balancing their needs with those of their partners and children. They want to be faithful to the call of love that forms the basis of spirituality.

Women who felt led to stay may wonder what God was about. Why would God ask them to pay such a high price for faithfulness? Why would God allow them to be betrayed so many times, to have their hopes dashed so tragically? Why didn't God protect them or at least give them the freedom to protect themselves? Many women may feel defeated and betrayed by God when the decision to leave finally breaks up their family and the marriage they tried so hard to maintain.

Some may wonder why God "made" this happen. I do not believe for one second that God wanted this outcome for me or for anyone else. The definition of evil is that which is against the will of God—choices made against love. God allows people to exercise freedom, even when that freedom is used to go against goodness. Yet God remains with those who *choose* to hurt and those who *are* hurt.

ASSESSING THE LIKELIHOOD
OF THE ABUSER'S RECOVERY

Many abusers promise to change when the threat of divorce is upon them, and some abusers do change. Many of the men who dedicate themselves to work in domestic abuse grew up in abusive homes and have worked hard to change the patterns they learned growing up.

However, the recovery rate is depressingly low. Abusers are notoriously manipulative. They have practiced deceiving their partners through countless repetitions of the abuse cycle: honeymoon/deception, tension, and crisis.

Abusers vary in their response to a woman's decision to leave a relationship. Some immediately escalate threats and punishment. Some abruptly abandon their partners and find another woman. Some make a preemptive move toward divorce to gain financial advantage. Many promise to change. The most accomplished use all the above strategies in confusing combinations. The threat of a potential end to the relationship launches many into an intense version of the honeymoon/deception phase.

"Ana" told her husband "Oscar" that she was ready for divorce two years before they actually separated. She was serious, but she also dreaded the thought of breaking up her family. Apparently desperate, Oscar promised he could change—that it was really just a matter of making a solid decision. He claimed he had quit smoking cold turkey and swore he could do the same with his anger. Against all reason, she agreed to give it a try. For six weeks he was wonderful. Oscar had the skills to be funny, thoughtful, helpful, and attentive. He turned them on. After six weeks, Ana finally began to think Oscar might actually pull it off—that previous failures sprang just from a lack of real resolve on his part. As soon as she began to relax, the downward slide began.

They went through the cycle several more times that year. Each six-week honeymoon was based on some promised change. Oscar promised to try medication, then to actually take the medication, then to attend a Parents Anonymous group, then to find a sponsor, then to actually see the sponsor, then to try anger management classes. Each cycle was identical: wonderful behavior for six weeks, then a gradual slide into old patterns. Ana finally caught on and didn't relax after six weeks; the final "honeymoon" lasted ten weeks. As they were going to bed one night, Ana told Oscar that she thought he had finally changed and she might be able to trust him. With a warm smile he responded, "Why don't you just relax?" The downward slide began the next day.

Professionals who work with abusers are trained never to take their statements at face value. Many therapists require abusers to sign releases allowing the counselor to speak with partners; without such outside verification, it is difficult to judge whether abusers are making real progress.

Michael Paymar, of the Oakland Men's Project, says that typically when men begin treatment programs the physical violence decreases but the controlling behaviors increase.[10] How can a woman tell if a man is honestly working a recovery program or lying? According to Paymar, there is no way of telling up front which men will recover. Men who are initially hostile and resistant sometimes make dramatic changes, while other men who are articulate and apparently cooperative simply become more sophisticated in abuse and deception.

Even an abuser who is honestly working a recovery program may relapse. Long-term recovery is never guaranteed. However, there are certain markers that indicate an abuser is making real changes. The absence of these markers is the equivalent to smelling beer on an alcoholic; in spite of his protests to the contrary, the abuser is not in recovery.

An abuser who is honestly working a recovery program will:

1. *Clearly acknowledge and take responsibility for his behavior, his intentions while abusing, and the consequences of his abuse.* This will take time, as the abuser gradually works through the denial with which he has shrouded his choices. Many abusers "forget" past behavior or may acknowledge behavior in the distant past while denying recent behavior. To be trustworthy, this acknowledgment needs to remain consistent over time.

2. *Recognize he has a lifelong problem.* An abuser who says, "I used to have a problem with anger but I dealt with it," is unlikely to be in recovery. This is equivalent to saying, "I used to be an alcoholic." Men who have been abusive for any length of time have extremely powerful ingrained responses to stress and uncertainty. The true question is whether he is actively working on recovery. Like alcoholics, abusers need to live in the knowledge, "My name is _____, and I am an abuser."

3. *Respect boundaries.* Abusers will often claim not to understand why a woman needs boundaries; therefore they feel no responsibility to honor them. Someone who is in recovery will acknowledge the need to respect boundaries even if he does not understand or agree with the need for them.

4. *Make amends.* One method of making amends and a helpful tool for maintaining recovery is for an abuser to tell the truth about his behavior to key people. Many abusers are so manipulative they can "confess" their past in such a way that listeners walk away feeling sorry for them. An abuser demonstrates sincerity and increases his chances for maintaining recovery if he acknowledges the truth to his children, close friends, and an ongoing circle of people who understand abuse. Abusers do not need sympathy, which becomes enabling. They need people (in addition to their partners) who have compassion for them but will still hold them accountable for their actions. An abuser who is serious about taking responsibility for his own recovery will seek out these people in his life.

5. *Refrain from revenge or trashtalking about his partner or other people.* No one is perfect, and everyone can be critical, but until a pattern of vindictive actions and words against anyone has been broken, the abuser is unlikely to be a safe partner.

6. *Refrain from "victim talk."* Even the most vicious abuser sees himself as a victim. His perception of himself as a victim causes him to lack empathy for others and gives him internal permission to do terrible things. An abuser who sees himself primarily as a

victim at work, with friends, or in any other setting is at serious risk for backsliding. Some men are skilled at creating an impression that they have been victimized by an ex-partner without ever making direct allegations against her.

7. *Be deliberate about his choice of friends.* One of the painful parts of recovering from alcoholism is leaving behind friendships with active alcoholics. It is difficult for men to maintain recovery if they spend significant time with people who see them as victims or who are themselves abusive. An abuser who is serious about recovery will recognize the power of the feedback he receives in his life and seek out friends who are respectful and reflect the new reality he is trying to enter.

Recovery takes time and progress will be uneven. An Al-Anon member said of alcoholics, "It takes them two years to get their brains out of hock and three more to learn how to use them." Recovery is slow, slow, slow. But without an *overall* progression toward health, old patterns will inevitably return. Survivors need to be very sensitive to the dynamics of power within their relationship and not give back power to a partner who is untrustworthy.

GATHERING THE NECESSARY RESOURCES TO LEAVE

Leaving an abusive relationship can be extremely dangerous, even if the abuser has not shown a high level of previous physical violence. If at all possible, women should get advice from a domestic abuse therapist or from staff at a battered women's shelter. Advice tailored to the situation and the support of at least one caring person are extremely important to make a victim's transition as safe as possible. This book deals more with the emotional than the practical aspects of recovery. Books and agencies listed in the resource section can provide the victim with the support she needs to make the best choices she can. Key elements are developing a safety plan, getting financial and legal information and advice, and finding emotional support.

Virtually all abusers engage in some form of harassment when a partner leaves. For some, this period is extremely unsafe. Unless absolutely necessary, a woman should not leave without a plan. She must not let embarrassment or a reluctance to become one of "those women" get in the way of her getting the help she needs. Underestimating the escalation that may occur from her partner if she decides to leave, with or without telling him in advance, could be very dangerous.

The process of leaving will vary depending on the abuser. It is very difficult to leave without support, and some abusers successfully cut their partners off from all outside resources. Immigrant and rural women are at particular risk for this isolation.

Understanding help *is* available. Local shelters, Internet sites, and private therapists can provide guidance in developing a safety plan. An abuser will probably feel threatened if he knows a partner is thinking of leaving; Leaving a relationship is the ultimate affront to an abuser, and an enraged abuser should never be underestimated.

Informed help is a vital resource in successfully making the transition out of an abusive relationship. Whenever possible, escape should be cautious, carefully planned, and done with the aid of skilled outside help.

3

Coping with Harassment

Unless a man takes separation as an opportunity to honestly work a recovery program, abuse usually escalates as a woman tries to end a relationship. When I asked Laura, my therapist, what percentage of her clients experienced harassment after leaving their partners, she paused for a moment, perplexed. Then she responded, "Well, all of them." She gave it a little more thought and then said, "I can't think of anyone who hasn't. It takes different forms—sometimes it's physical, sometimes it's through the family, sometimes it's financial. But it's always there."

STALKING AND HARASSMENT

Attorney and author Dawn Bradley Berry defines stalking as "any pattern of behavior that serves no legitimate purpose and is intended to harass, annoy or terrorize the victim."[11] Patricia Tjaden and Nancy Thoennes, in their brief on the National Violence Against Women Survey, say,

Stalking generally refers to harassing or threatening behavior that an individual engages in repeatedly, such as following a person, appearing at a person's home or place of business, making harassing phone calls, leaving written messages or objects, or vandalizing a person's property. These actions may or may not be accompanied by a credible threat of serious harm, and they may or may not be precursors to an assault or murder. . . . Most states define stalking as the willful, malicious and repeated following and harassing of another person.[12]

Stalking is governed by state laws, which are being revised as the understanding of stalking improves. The model antistalking code developed by the National Institute of Justice does not require stalkers to make a credible threat of violence against victims, but it does require victims to feel a high level of fear of bodily harm. Hopefully this code will continue to be refined to include any fear of harm that is precipitated by the abuser's current and past pattern of behavior.

To be effective, laws must be enforced by persons who understand the aftermath of abuse and the complex and subtle ways in which many abusers threaten their former partners. For example, there is no specific law against leaving roadkill at a woman's front door. A pet tragically killed by a passing motorist has no sinister meaning in itself. And yet, as part of a pattern of stalking, these happenings may indicate very serious danger.

In conversation, people generally use the term "harassment" to mean continued unwanted contact and "stalking" to indicate a clear intention to threaten physical harm. While stalking carries greater physical risk, the ongoing intrusion of harassment can also have a powerful impact on a survivor. The difference is a matter of degree rather than substance; as with abuse, the intention is to control and punish a partner. The essence of stalking or harassment is not revealed in any one incident, but through pattern and persistence.

PREVALENCE AND IMPACT

Stalking and harassment have only recently begun to be recognized as serious problems. California was the first state to pass an antistalking law in 1990, and law enforcement agencies only recently began collecting data about stalking. The National Violence Against Women Survey, cosponsored by the National Institute of Justice and the Centers for Disease Control and Prevention, indicates that over a million women are stalked annually in the United States. Fifty-nine percent of these incidents are committed by intimate partners, and only about half of all stalking victims seek help from law enforcement. Women said they did not contact police because (a) they did not consider it appropriate, (b) they thought the police would be unable to help, or (c) they were afraid of reprisals.

Thirty percent of women who have been stalked reported seeking psychological help to cope with their experience, and 26 percent reported losing time from work as a result of being harassed. One in five women who reported being stalked moved to a new home in an attempt to escape from the threat. Only 18 percent of women reported that stalking ceased when their partner found a new relationship.[13]

Harassment and stalking are enormously powerful weapons. Perhaps only those who have experienced them can understand the impact. The oppressive sense of ongoing threat interferes with a woman's ability to engage in and enjoy life even though the relationship with her partner has theoretically ended.

The National Violence Against Women Survey outlines the severity of the problem and presents some recommendations for more effective responses. First, stalking should be treated as both a criminal justice problem and a public health concern. Also, the "credible threat" requirement should be removed from antistalking statutes, since so many stalkers are extremely skilled at ducking legal repercussions. This would create broader protection for women living in emotional rather than physical danger. The survey also establishes a solid link between stalking and physical assault, which supports a more proactive criminal justice approach to the issue. Since 70 percent of all restraining orders are violated, the survey recommends further investigation of effective intervention on the part of police. And finally, mental health professionals should receive better training on stalking and its impact on victims' mental health. The wisdom of these recommendations offers hope to women subjected to harassment.

ANTICIPATING HARASSMENT

Many women expect retaliation when they leave their partners. An abuser will often try to hold on to a partner by threatening to harm her, her children, or himself. Women are wise to assume it will be risky to end the relationship.

Some women do not anticipate harassment. "Latisha's" parents had an extremely difficult marriage but a cooperative divorce. Her family had peaceful blended holidays and family events for ten years after her parents' marriage ended. Latisha expected the same when she and her husband parted. She waited to leave the marriage until she was exhausted and convinced there was no hope, assuming that divorce would provide safety. She was completely wrong.

The separation initiated a whole new round of abuse that caught Latisha utterly by surprise. It was months before she could fully comprehend what was happening to her, and more than three years before she was able to handle it effectively. Better information would have helped her move more quickly and with less collateral damage.

Outsiders rarely understand harassment and so have trouble believing it is occurring. Even people who care deeply about a woman may have trouble supporting her because of their lack of awareness. In addition to this confusion, there is an oppressive darkness to stalking and harassment that tempts bystanders to want to deny and avoid conflict.

This lack of comprehension makes victims more vulnerable. Understanding harassment is a major step toward protecting women and their children and reducing the likelihood that abuse will continue into the next generation. Access to information about harassment can reduce the cost of their former partners' behavior. Learning how to survive and cope with harassment is critical to a woman's ability to escape abuse and heal herself and her life.

WHY DOES HARASSMENT OCCUR?

When a relationship ends, the abuser finds himself in a spot much like an alcoholic who runs out of gin. The important difference is that an alcoholic can walk into any liquor store and buy what he needs. An abuser does not have this freedom—he is dependent on someone else to provide him with his fix. His high comes from inflicting abuse and from self-pity. Abusers are often extremely dependent on their partners and crave access to them in order to try to wrest from them the self-esteem they lack. Because they feel entitled to their partners' submission, they feel deprived when it becomes unavailable. Many also put great effort into seeking out people who will join them in denial and provide sympathy to reinforce their misguided beliefs.

An abuser without a partner has no satisfactory outlet for his frustrations until he is able to find a new relationship. While some abusers are aggressive in work or social environments, they usually do not enjoy the same power in those settings as at home. An abuser with a well-established cycle will experience intense discomfort when unable to engage in abuse for an extended period of time, much like an alcoholic's withdrawal. His discomfort may approach the level of panic if it appears his partner will succeed in escaping the relationship.

If abuse was kept hidden from outsiders, men may fear that separation and/or divorce will reveal the secret to outsiders. Shame is an intense emotion, and fear of being exposed can be a powerful catalyst for abusers. Harassment often is intended to intimidate the victim into keeping the secret and punish her if she refuses.

DANGERS AND COSTS OF HARASSMENT

Abusers who did not engage in much physical violence during a relationship may escalate to serious assault and even murder when a partner attempts to escape. In a recent year in Milwaukee, every woman murdered by an intimate partner had already separated from him.

Women often wait to divorce or leave a partner until their emotional resources are virtually exhausted. Their depleted state makes coping with harassment particularly difficult. Women who reach their breaking point before leaving the relationship may suffer long-term damage as a result of the additional trauma of harassment. Their ability to parent effectively and successfully navigate their lives may be seriously and permanently impaired. Women who are being stalked often lose time from work, and some may even lose their jobs. Stalking is costly.

Even women who are aware of the dangers of leaving may be unprepared for the severity or duration of the harassment. Stalking lasts for an average of 2.2 years. Stalking by intimate partners in a long-term relationship typically lasts longer. Author David Decker suggests that if harassment lasts more than two years and persists after an abuser develops a relationship with another woman, it will probably be a lifelong pattern. That is very discouraging news.

Some men lose interest in harassing a former partner when they enter a new relationship, but many men continue to disturb former partners while pursuing a relationship with another woman. This combination of hostility and infidelity can be particularly painful.

GOALS OF STALKING AND HARASSMENT

Many of the goals and strategies of harassment are part of the pattern of abuse that occurred while the relationship was intact. Some abusers develop new methods that they did not consider necessary before the breakup. These strategies may take a different form to adapt to changing circumstances or may become more prominent in the absence of the day-to-day relationship. The emergence of new strategies is unnerving for women and can be very confusing for children. Unpredictability can further complicate family relationships, compromising a woman's emotional strength and making positive parenting more difficult.

In the beginning, women can be simply bewildered, stunned, and confused by their partners' behavior. As months pass, they begin to discover patterns. Actions that at first seemed pointless or incomprehensible begin to make sense once they understand their partner's intentions. Understanding increases their ability to cope with and manage the harassment. Stalking and harassment are not accidental, nor are they the result of blind rage. They are deliberate and purposeful, with a series of very specific goals:

- to isolate and discredit the victim,
- to be perceived as a victim to gain sympathy,
- to be perceived as a "good guy" and render ongoing abuse unbelievable,
- to retain and continue to use opportunities to punish and control the victim,
- to prevent the victim from moving on and developing a new life, and
- to enlist others in inflicting punishment on the victim.

TO ISOLATE AND DISCREDIT THE VICTIM

Isolation is a classic strategy of abusers. By isolating the victim, the abuser is able to gain greater power over her. Human beings are most vulnerable when alone, and those who have already been terrorized feel their aloneness and vulnerability with particular intensity.

By isolating and marginalizing a woman, the abuser is better able to attack her credibility. Many women have become isolated emotionally, if not physically, by the time they leave a relationship. If the abuser is connected with family and community members, people may feel bonded and loyal to him and out of touch with his victim. They may blame her for initiating a divorce or breakup. This makes it less likely that a victim's voice will be heard even if she does speak up. It also reduces the likelihood that people will reach out to support her, leaving her even more alone and vulnerable. Cathy Hartle, executive director for the Hands of Hope Resource Center in Minnesota, says, "Oftentimes the batterer will rely on the community thinking it's about [the woman]. He's out there recruiting. . . . This is probably a sad comment, but they can generally get a lot of support for what they do to their women."[14]

A divorcing couple was employed by the same company. The husband had been known for being abrasive with coworkers and defiant toward administrators and had no friends on staff, but when the couple parted he suddenly became the social secretary of the organization. He was transformed: accommodating in his work and charming in the hallways and lunchroom. He flirted with younger staff members and frequently sent out humorous if somewhat inappropriate group e-mails inviting employees to after-hours gatherings at local restaurants and bars. Without ever saying a negative word about his ex-wife, he managed to marginalize her and create an enormously painful environment for her in her workplace.

Women may be traumatized to the point of confusion and have difficulty thinking and expressing themselves clearly. Fear and loneliness increase their anxiety, resentment, and neediness, characteristics people often find unappealing or even repellent. Victims instinctively know this, find these qualities unattractive in themselves, and have even more difficulty reaching out to ask for and find support. In the above situation, it was natural for people to respond to the husband's pleasantries—and to consciously or unconsciously avoid intimate conversation with the wife.

The shame that causes many women to hide abuse compounds their dilemma. If they have kept the secret for years, it is difficult to begin to talk about what is happening—and difficult for people to find this new story believable.

To Be Perceived as a Victim to Gain Sympathy

Abusers justify their behavior by seeing themselves as victims. They feel sorry for themselves and often want others to feel sorry for them too. This is frequently an attempt to compensate for healthy nurturing they did not receive as children. Many abusers are incredibly skillful at manipulating people into commiserating with them and so substitute sympathy for real intimacy.

Abusers may express tremendous sorrow to outsiders at the end of the relationship, while at the same time directing only anger and hostility toward their partners. If they can convince others they have been victimized, the woman is then seen as being to blame and a "reasonable" target of punishment. One woman's ex-husband, an attorney, told their friends he had purchased a new house for her. This was untrue; in reality she repeatedly found herself in court trying to collect support payments that he never made.

Tenderhearted but uninformed friends can do serious damage at this stage. It is often easier to enable someone than to confront with compassion. Many abusers, like alcoholics, only choose recovery if they hit bottom. Seeing an abuser as a victim helps remove the bottom and lessens the likelihood of recovery. The price is paid not only by an abuser's partner, but by his children, his future partners, and by the abuser himself.

To Be Perceived as a "Good Guy" and Render Ongoing Abuse Unbelievable

Some abusers have excellent social skills that they turn on and off at will. They may present an affable, engaging manner to outsiders in order to enlist them in denial of ongoing abuse. Many abusers are active in church and community work, sometimes as a means of deflecting suspicion. Michelle Weldon's husband volunteered as a Big Brother, publicly posing as a positive role model, while punching his wife at home. One church pastor beat his wife and threw another woman off a balcony while staying in active ministry. Many abusers want to deflect their own awareness of their actions and will work hard to convince themselves that they are harmless. They may present themselves as caring friends and loving fathers, although their actual attachment to friends and families is usually very limited.

Because the "Jekyll and Hyde" personality is unfamiliar and unbelievable to those who have not witnessed it in action, outsiders—and sometimes even abusers' children—are unlikely to suspect or believe that harassment continues. The abuser may present himself as concerned for his partner's welfare; in public he may act hurt that she blocks his attempts to contact her. "Graciela's" husband repeatedly contacted her family and friends, asking how she was doing and why she wouldn't speak with him, while simultaneously harassing and terrifying her.

To Retain and Continue to Use Opportunities to Punish and Control the Victim

Because abusers use aggressive behavior as a primary means of discharging tension, anxiety, and unhappiness, they cling to their opportunities to abuse. Abusers who are relatively appropriate in other adult relationships have a particular investment in maintaining access to an estranged partner since they have no other place to vent their discomfort.

Abusers who operate in a culture where men are expected to dominate women risk losing face if their partners leave. This is a powerful source of shame for them and can prompt drastic actions.

When women decide to leave a relationship they upset the established balance of power. This enrages the abuser, who may use any means at his disposal to reestablish power and control to take revenge on his partner.

To Prevent the Victim from Moving On and Developing a New Life

An abuser desperately wants to force his partner to stay in the relationship and to disable her efforts to build a new life apart from him. Some men put the agenda clearly on the table, declaring, "If I can't have you no one else will." These men may kill a former partner if she becomes involved with someone else or physically disfigure her so she will be unattractive to other men.

A counselor asked "Nate" why he tried to restrict his wife from going out socially and why he required her to call home frequently if she did. Nate responded, "I don't want her to be able to forget about us. I want her to always be thinking about us." The abuser wants to be a constant presence in his partner's brain.

Stalking creates ongoing destabilization for a woman. New incidents knock her off balance, leaving her exhausted, terrified, and depressed. Recovery may take years after leaving a partner. During that time there may be many days when she is distraught, weeping, anxious, and distracted. She may overreact to conflict or rejection in other relationships. She can be hard to be around, and her relationship with her children may be strained as a result.

This can be stressful on a woman's relationships with family and friends, and can make finding new friendships exceptionally difficult. It certainly does not help her to be a lighthearted, fun dating prospect. Each time a new incident throws a woman off balance, there is added frustration in knowing her partner has won yet another victory. Harassment slows a woman's progress toward freedom—but she *can* make progress.

To Enlist Others in Inflicting Punishment

If an abuser is successful in isolating and discrediting his partner, he may also be able to get others to join in punishing her. Family and community members often find a victim's presence uncomfortable, especially if she gives any signs of distress. Acknowledging the abuse would upset the community status quo, which is comfortable or at least familiar. A woman's pain or protest disturbs the tranquility of the group, and members may respond by shunning her or engaging in other types of punishment to silence her or drive her out of the community.

Searching for a new place where she could worship free of her former husband's presence, "Abby" visited a neighboring parish for Mass. On her first visit she unexpectedly encountered her former husband's aunt and uncle. She left her pew as they passed her going down the aisle. When she greeted them his aunt's face took on an expression of absolute disgust; she refused to look at or speak to Abby. An active and committed Catholic, Abby had to move on yet again in her search for a parish where she could worship in peace.

This type of community response is not specific to domestic abuse. Women who have been raped, people of color who are the targets of racism, and others who experience injustice find similar responses. The horrifying news stories of sexual abuse by clergy in the Catholic Church mirror this dynamic. Perpetrators and those who protect them with a conspiracy of silence can be found everywhere. Those who break the silence often suffer serious reprisals.

DISTINGUISHING BETWEEN OVERT AND COVERT HARASSMENT

Some men make no effort to hide their actions and may intimidate bystanders as well as their partners. Such *overt harassment* is clearly obvious to outsiders. Harassment is more likely to be overt in cultural settings where violence and abuse of women are considered normal, though some men will use intimidation in any setting. "Carla's" husband strode into a bingo hall where she was out with relatives, his behavior so obviously dangerous that staff arranged a safe escort for her to her car.

Particularly in situations where violence is considered unacceptable, men may engage in more subtle means of intimidation. This is called *covert harassment*. Abusers who are skilled in manipulation can create an atmosphere of terror without resorting to outright physical intimidation. They often enlist bystanders to help them.

As educational levels rise and people become more adept at verbal manipulation, covert harassment is becoming more common. Many men engage in covert harassment that is invisible to outsiders but extremely destructive to their partners. Their abuse may have been overt before separation, when they were living at home without outside observers. These same men may become experts at covertly harassing a partner, continuing to make life miserable while escaping notice by outsiders.

When confronted, abusers protest their innocence and give excuses that on the surface may seem plausible. Covert abusers engage in great internal denial of their intentions. The truth is discovered by looking at the pattern of incidents. While covert harassment may be confusing, at its heart the goal is the same: to control and punish.

WORDS AND ACTIONS IN
CONFLICT: COGNITIVE DISSONANCE

Abuse is difficult for victims not simply because it is directly painful and frightening but also because many abusers' words and behavior are so seriously out of alignment that the discrepancy causes terror. Cognitive dissonance occurs when what a woman knows does not correspond with what she sees or experiences.

A man may pound on his partner's locked apartment door, threatening and cursing, trying to break in. The next morning she will find a bouquet of flowers on the front seat of her locked car. The scene in the apartment hallway is obviously hostile. The violation of her personal space to leave the flowers is equally threatening, even though flowers appear to be a sign of affection. The stark contrast between the two interactions is frightening in itself.

Men who engage in covert harassment become expert at behavior that is menacing but *appears* innocuous. There is something inherently terrifying about the contrast between word and intention. Because victims of abuse already have distorted internal warning systems, which overreact to some threats and fail to recognize others altogether, this dynamic is particularly destructive.

One day, when "Sara" was particularly distraught over her husband's harassment, she left him a voice message begging him to stop contacting her. He immediately voice-mailed back, profusely apologetic, professing his concern for her and promising to absolutely leave her alone. Five hours later he was in her house with her son. The contrast between words and actions tempts a woman to feel as though she is crazy, when the dysfunction is actually on the other side.

Like the criminal who leaves a distinguishing clue behind to taunt law enforcement officers, an abuser may go out of his way to covertly frighten his victim while she is in the presence of others. She is with people who have the potential to help her, but she knows she will be seen as overreacting, vindictive, or disruptive if she objects to what is going on. Because of her former husband's harassment, "Amy" left Cursillo, a wonderful religious movement that had been an important part of her life for thirty years. Later she signed up to work on a Cursillo retreat offered in Spanish, a language she spoke but her former husband did not. He promptly signed up to serve in the kitchen. When she asked him to remove himself from the team, an old friend also working the kitchen team informed Amy that she "needed help."

To an uninformed person, the abuser's behavior may appear not only innocent but also caring. Men commonly send flowers to estranged partners at their workplace, knowing both that the woman has forbidden the gift and that coworkers will see the bouquet as a sign of his love. One man wallpapered his former wife's kitchen while she was out of town. Persistent unwanted gifts are a symbol of power, not love. Outsiders' misperceptions of the relationship contribute to the sense of unreality and powerlessness that threatens a victim's world.

STRATEGIES OF STALKING AND HARASSMENT

Abusers use a variety of methods to stalk their partners. Strategies are tailored to the circumstances, the personalities of the couple, and previous patterns of abuse. Here are a few common strategies:

- using physical violence,
- crossing boundaries,
- accelerating instances of harassment,
- using money to manipulate, and
- using the children to manipulate.

USING PHYSICAL VIOLENCE

An abuser may use physical violence or the threat of violence in an attempt to force the victim to stay in the relationship or to punish her for leaving. Men may threaten or use physical violence against their partners, children, extended family, pets, or themselves. They may threaten symbolically, by leaving a bouquet of dead roses or a defaced photograph on their victim's desk. Physical violence is the most clearly dangerous, and most straightforward, strategy available to abusers. Horrific stories are common and go largely unnoticed in the newspaper.

CROSSING BOUNDARIES

An abuser crosses boundaries in order to frighten his partner and because he feels entitled to maintain contact and control. He intends to remind his victim that there is no escape, that the abuser continues to have access to her that he will use when he chooses. Finding ways to get past boundaries can become a game for the abuser. Taking his victim by surprise and contacting her by a variety of means and in a variety of settings contributes to her sense of vulnerability and his sense of power.

Some men create the illusion of being omnipresent, producing a pervasive sense of constant terror in their partners. As a woman struggles with the transition of ending her relationship and perhaps caring for children, she may despair of ever having a normal life.

Boundaries are crossed *overtly* when an abuser makes hostile or threatening phone calls or forcibly enters a house or workplace. An abuser may make many telephone calls in rapid succession to disrupt a work or home environment. He may break into a woman's home or vandalize her property. It is estimated that three-fourths of all abuse victims are harassed at work. Women experiencing overt harassment may have access to some legal support and protection, although restraining orders and orders of protection often have little impact and may even make a situation worse.

Boundaries are crossed *covertly* when an abuser makes persistent and unnecessary contact using children or other pretexts. An abuser may be very skillful in using a woman's reluctance to confront his violations in front of their children or in public as a means of rendering her more helpless. Women experiencing covert harassment generally are unable to use legal protection and have greater difficulty getting support and understanding from others. Even concerned and informed attorneys and police personnel may be unable to help her.

ACCELERATING INSTANCES OF HARASSMENT

Stalking and harassment often follow the same type of cyclical pattern established during the relationship. Each cycle begins with smaller, less frequent incidents and accelerates to more serious incidents spaced more closely together. There may be breaks between episodes. My former husband's episodes generally lasted two to four months, with breaks that lasted four to six weeks. Just as I began to think the harassment was over, a new cycle would begin.

An accelerating pattern of harassment adds to a woman's terror. This acceleration has the effect of linking incidents together and rendering them more powerful. Each incident is traumatic in its own right but also warns of future events. She not only experiences the pain, fear, or humiliation of the current incident but also remembers previous incidents and anticipates future incidents, which she knows are coming and will be more painful, frightening, or humiliating. The sense of helplessness in the face of this progression is very debilitating.

A woman's sensitivity to this dynamic is heightened by her experience while in the relationship. The cycle of honeymoon/tension/explosion is very familiar, and by the time she leaves she is highly attuned to her partner's patterns and alert to threatening signals. Once she is no longer living with him, she may become even more uneasy because she cannot observe the warning signs. The mounting tension of the cycle tempts her to make contact with the abuser and protest, thus reinforcing the pattern. Eventually even infrequent incidents of harassment can produce a constant state of intense fear.

Using Money to Manipulate

Money is a source and symbol of power, and abusers often use it to get and keep control over their partners. Men who are overtly abusive may hide income, refuse to pay child support or maintenance, run up large debts before or during separation, or engage in unnecessary and costly legal battles. They may make unexpected and malicious changes in insurance coverage or property ownership, or withhold necessary information from a partner to punish her or force her to make contact with him.

Men who engage in covert harassment will toy with money by being unpredictable in making payments or slightly reducing support payments to remind the victim of her financial vulnerability. A proactive approach and an attorney who is competent in dealing with abusive partners can be of enormous help in protecting against these actions. Local women's resource centers or domestic abuse agencies may be able to provide referrals to lawyers skilled in this area.

USING THE CHILDREN TO MANIPULATE

Abusers may use their own children to manipulate their victims. Overt harassment includes frightening, harming, threatening, or even kidnapping children in order to intimidate and control a partner. A childcare worker told me of a man who kidnapped his toddler from a day care center and threatened to disappear unless his wife took him back. Children are extremely vulnerable to this type of action, both because of their size and because so much of their day is spent in the company of other children or with adults who are not alert to their danger. The threat of harm to her children causes enormous anxiety and pain for a mother and is a powerful lever for control. Because abusers typically have very limited empathy or real love for anyone, they are capable of brutal action toward helpless children, a fact their partners know only too well.

Covert abusers are more likely to attempt to win over children and alienate them from their mother. Men who were abusive to their children while living at home may change their style when they leave. Since they no longer have to deal with the disruption, frustration, and inconvenience of day-to-day parenting, they may find it easier to be pleasant. They may have greater financial resources and can "buy" children's affection. This may look like a change in character when in fact it is simply a shift in circumstances.

Some men have little contact with their children and then years later reenter their lives, welcomed by children hungry for love. Very often this reentry is motivated simply by a desire to further harass the mother or to impress a new partner. Some may use the new relationship with their children to deliberately reduce the time children spend with their mothers, knowing this will cause her pain.

An abuser may attempt to win over his children in order to reinforce his own denial. If the couple's children see the father as no longer abusive, this is used as compelling evidence that harassment is not occurring and the mother is overreacting or lying. Children who long for attention and affirmation from their fathers are strongly tempted to join him in this denial. An abuser who is successful in engaging his children in denial has seriously tipped the balance of power in his favor. Unfortunately, children who move into denial develop an additional obstacle to their own recovery and future healthy relationships.

In one well-publicized case, a man beat his wife so severely that she lost a kidney. When he received the hospital bill three days after her release, he beat her again. Years later, when she tried to divorce him, he strangled her in the process of kidnapping her. The assault caused a stroke that permanently disabled her arm. He disappeared with her to Mexico where he was discovered and arrested three weeks later. Brought to trial, he was sentenced to fifteen years in prison. All of his adult children in the courtroom that day were dismayed at his sentence. None sat with their mother.[15]

Even mothers who would like their children to experience affirmation from their fathers want to cry out at this dishonesty. They may watch abusers reviving a relationship with their children while simultaneously failing to make child support payments or taking other action harmful to the children's welfare.

"Darrell" initiated a renewed relationship with one of his teenage daughters who was living at home with her mother. He decided to give "Becky" a car, something his other four children had never received. However, he kept the car in his name and did not add her to his insurance policy. His former wife, "Tracy," could not insure her daughter, since the car belonged to her husband. Becky desperately wanted the car, and her father assured her she did not need insurance. Darrell finally added his daughter to his policy when Tracy notified him she would not allow the car to be driven or parked in her driveway without insurance. For a time, Becky saw her father as a hero for taking care of her and believed Tracy was blocking her freedom out of overprotectiveness and spite.

Many women stay in an abusive marriage because they see it as a seriously flawed but preferable alternative for their children's welfare. Even if the decision to stay was a mistake, women have suffered in their attempts to care for their children and are highly invested in their relationship with them. Since most often the mother is the custodial parent, she must deal with the normal periods of alienation that occur with disciplining children and setting boundaries for them. In addition, she is parenting children who are experiencing family disruption and have witnessed or experienced abuse. Some days the additional conflict created by the malicious interference of a former partner seems too much to bear.

Grief and outrage at a partner's manipulation may lead to conflict between a mother and her children. It also reduces a woman's ability to be an effective help to her children at a time when they desperately need support and guidance. Outside assistance is particularly important in navigating this challenge.

THE GIFT OF CLARITY

As horrendous and dangerous as stalking can be, it holds one important gift: clarity. Over time, harassment reveals the stark reality of the abuser's intentions and character, leading his victim to see who he *really* is.

"Rosa" stayed in her marriage partly because she thought "Carlos" wanted to change but lacked the necessary personal and professional resources. His rage seemed to be triggered by stressful incidents such as being contradicted or having a child neglect his toys. Arguments between them were often unreasonable, but at least they happened within the context of a conversation. Once things got rolling Rosa became angry and often said regrettable things—responsibility for their conflict was not all one-sided.

Rosa knew they had not found the right professional help, but Carlos went to counseling willingly. He enjoyed talking about himself and liked the warm response he got from therapists. At the time it seemed to be a lack of initiative that kept him locked in old patterns. He did not look for classes or books to help him grow, but he did not take classes or read books on other topics either.

During their final two years together, it became obvious that simple inertia was not the issue. Carlos's repeated and consistent failure to follow through on his promises was clearly motivated by a desire to maintain his freedom to abuse. Each cycle brought that depressing truth home more clearly, although Rosa needed to have it hammered into her awareness many times before she was ready to act on it.

While they were married, Carlos alternated abuse with kind and apparently caring actions. When he bought flowers or made dinner Rosa knew abuse would follow, but Carlos seemed to also have some genuine love and concern for her and their children. His ongoing harassment after leaving caused her to reconsider her opinion. By the time they separated she was terrified of conflict with him; after a few months of harassment she was terrified of any contact with him at all. He had lived with her through her gradual deterioration and knew how fragile she had become. In letters, telephone conversations, and sessions with his counselor, Rosa pleaded with him to leave her alone. But he kept on coming. She had all the disadvantages of divorce, but few of the advantages.

A significant part of the pain of harassment is a woman's growing realization of what the abuse from her partner has always been about. When an abuser is sometimes kind and attentive, a woman believes the love between them is somehow real, in spite of all the evidence to the contrary. Over time it becomes clear that a partner's hostility and intention to abuse doomed the relationship from the beginning. His priority has always been *his* perceived needs, not hers.

The pure hostility of stalking is hard to comprehend, particularly after years of a woman telling herself to forgive and try to see the positive in her partner. But harassment presents her with a clear opportunity to recognize the negative as her partner becomes more and more ingenious in finding ways to make contact. I commented to abuse counselor Dave Decker that the harassment was harder to bear than the original abuse, because it seemed so calculated. Dave quickly responded, "I would submit it has *all* been calculated." It took a year and a half of harassment before I was able to truly grasp that fact.

Courageous women who have survived and grown wise and strong by traveling through this valley are powerful examples for abused women everywhere. Stalking is enormously oppressive. It carries a spiritual darkness as well as a sense of emotional vulnerability. The knowledge that her abuser is out there, circling her, intent on punishing his victim for protecting herself, carries a spiritual as well as a psychological impact.

For me, knowing that God was with me, even though he did not protect me on a practical level, was a source of strength. As I look back, I realize I needed every shred of help and hope I could find to survive this stretch. As bleak as the outlook may seem some days, it helps to remember that a victim does not walk the road alone. Someone is with her, and her abuser, even on the darkest days.

Part Two

Taking Back Your Life

Deciding to end a relationship is the beginning of a long, painful process. When your relationship is abusive, there are additional steps in the journey. Protecting yourself and healing from the ravages of abuse, breaking the isolation that is its inevitable result, grieving and letting go of the relationship, and building a new life are all necessary before you can be truly free. These tasks are difficult and take time, but through them you have the power to transform your pain and losses into wisdom and strength for the rest of your life. You can become a survivor.

The first part of this book focused on understanding your abuser and taking the first step away from him. The rest of this book deals primarily with you and your recovery. Recovering from an abusive relationship is like peeling an onion. Removing one layer only reveals another underneath. Beneath that is yet another layer that cannot be touched until the earlier ones are processed. As these layers are detached, your ability to forgive increases. As you are able to forgive and let go of bitterness, new grief will emerge. Boundaries that were hard and rigid because of your fragility may soften with the passage of time—or boundaries that are inadequate may need to be reinforced.

Recovery doesn't happen in a set, logical order. Each survivor tackles it in her own way. The following pages describe issues that are so thoroughly intertwined with abusive relationships that some repetition is inevitable. Feel free to read the chapters in whatever order seems helpful. You may find yourself rereading some sections as time passes. The section on grieving, for example, may carry one message soon after you separate from your partner and touch your heart in another way after you have been healed of some of your trauma.

Recovery is not easy. If it were, fewer women would be suffering today. But recovery *is* possible—if you find the right resources and are willing to do the work. The following chapters discuss three important tasks: learning to protect yourself, letting go of trying to control your partner, and learning to reach out and connect with trustworthy people and with God.

4

Setting Boundaries

When it comes to establishing boundaries, detaching, and trusting again, women face a chicken-and-egg dilemma. Which comes first? It is difficult to do one without the others. A step forward in one will increase a woman's capacity to progress in another; while neglecting one area will hamper her ability to move forward elsewhere. Building relationships with trustworthy people gives her strength to maintain boundaries; secure boundaries help her let go of trying to control people in her life. Practically speaking, she needs to make slow but steady progress in all three areas simultaneously.

Consider boundaries as a first step. Boundaries separate one entity from another, one country or state from another. They also separate human beings from one another. Boundaries help a woman sort out who she is and who the other person is—and isn't.

Dr. Henry Cloud and Dr. John Townsend, in their wonderful book *Boundaries: When to Say Yes, When to Say No, to Take Control of Your Life,* say that the function of boundaries is to keep in the good and keep out the bad.[16] Those who have experienced abuse have learned to do the opposite. Victims learn to let down their boundaries and allow abuse to be heaped on them. Then they absorb it and carry it around with them. Many women have also learned to shield themselves from letting good things come into their lives because of their fear of being vulnerable. They may have come to believe that they do not deserve to have good things and so block them when they come their way.

Boundaries are crossed when a legitimate "no" is not accepted. This happens when:

- A woman is touched against her will.
- She is insulted or demeaned.
- Her partner contacts her against her wishes.
- She is punished for making her own choices.

By definition, as long as a victim stays in an intimate relationship with her abuser, her boundaries will be violated. Abusers violate boundaries with their rage and violence, they violate boundaries sexually, and they violate boundaries with their neediness.

An abuser punishes his victim if she tries to maintain a sense of herself as a distinct person. She learns to suppress her instinct to protect herself because to do otherwise simply prolongs or intensifies the abuse. Arguing does not protect her; talking back is simply staying in the game. When a woman argues, she feels as though she is standing up for herself, but in reality she is helping maintain the status quo.[17] The easy way to test that theory is for a woman to ask herself: When the argument is over, has anything changed? Even if she "won" that particular debate, the level of abuse has not diminished. The only way to end the game is for the abuser to recover or for her to leave—really leave. The escalation that comes at the end of a relationship clearly illustrates that *truly* establishing a boundary is the ultimate affront to an abusive partner.

Over time, many women lose some awareness that their boundaries are being crossed and that they have a right to a different life. By the time many women leave their partners their internal warning systems have been shattered. A boundary is crossed and it may take days to figure out what happened. They are so accustomed to being violated that it seems normal to them. Some men's actions are blatant—they send threatening letters, pound on doors, call the workplace twenty times a day. In other cases the contacts are deceptive, done under pretext. Either way women feel frightened and distressed, but it is as if they are operating in a fog. Several days later they wake up and realize, "Wait a minute—he's not supposed to do that!"

Actions that are utterly transparent to an outsider can confuse and immobilize a recovering victim. While going through her divorce, "Linda" spent months trying to communicate to her estranged husband that she wanted no contact with him. One day he called to say the washing machine in his apartment building was not working and asked if he could do his laundry at her house. She was so frightened of him and had so thoroughly suppressed her healthy instincts that her mind went blank and she said yes. He came while she was at work and left papers and the remains of his lunch strewn across the kitchen table, making sure she was reminded of his presence when she walked in the door. It was not until days later that Linda realized it made no sense for him to have asked in the first place. The vulnerability and helplessness that come from the inability to recognize and stop boundary violations contribute to the fear that keeps women paralyzed.

Women are told that they simply need to develop internal strength so that their partners' actions won't bother them. Such condescension may make them want to scream, "But you don't understand!" Many women *cannot* stop reacting emotionally to their partners, at least in the beginning. Developing internal emotional boundaries is much easier if they can learn how to establish physical, external boundaries. They need a safe space in which to heal.

SETTING PHYSICAL BOUNDARIES

The first step toward healing is getting out of range of the abuse as much as possible. A victim who is being physically assaulted cannot heal unless she is able to remove her body from further harm. If at all possible, she needs to take practical steps to limit her abuser's ability to make contact while she works on her inner resistance. This can be especially difficult if she has children living with her who are in contact with their father. Doing all she can to set external boundaries helps her develop a sense of inner strength and control over her surroundings that will ultimately allow her to weather the inevitable difficult moments.

Many women have learned, either through faulty parenting when they were children or through society's messages to them as females, that it is not okay to protect themselves. They have learned that they must be nice, be accommodating, and do things simply because it is expected of them. Sometimes they accommodate others simply because they *think* it is expected. These messages have a powerful unconscious hold on them. Women have great difficulty saying no, even to unreasonable demands. They should follow certain steps to protect themselves. First, they need to give themselves permission to stand up for themselves and then develop strategies tailored to their particular situation.

Learning about assertive communication techniques can be helpful, although a woman will need to tailor the standard advice to her situation. A commonly taught communication format is:

(1) "When you _____ *[name a specific behavior], (2) I feel* _____ *[one or more emotions] (3) because* _____ *[give an explanation]. (4) Please* _____ *[make a specific request]. (5) If not, then* _____ *" [be prepared to impose a consequence].*

In setting boundaries with an abuser, it is usually best to omit the first three steps. The abuser's goal is to confuse, frighten, and hurt his victim, so the second step simply confirms that he is getting the payoff he seeks. A nonrecovering abuser is not interested in her explanations and is unlikely to change his behavior because of them. Going through the first three steps privately can be useful in helping a woman clarify her own thought processes. The key is deciding precisely what change she is looking for in her partner's behavior and what consequences she may be willing to give him that could have some kind of positive effect.

Like so many women, I thought that if I explained things really, really clearly, my husband would eventually get the message and leave me alone. He didn't. Two months after the divorce was final, I was still talking to him on the phone three and four times a day. I still remember my shock when Dave Decker suggested that I hang up when he called. I was familiar with imposing consequences when children failed to behave appropriately, but I was absolutely thunderstruck at the concept of giving consequences to an adult. It always seemed to me that adults should know, by their own code of ethics, what was appropriate behavior. I felt embarrassed holding an adult accountable, as though I were being impolite in calling attention to their actions. The thought of saying, "If you don't stop calling I will hang up on you," *and then following through*, was earthshaking.

Dave asked me why I *would not* hang up on my husband if I had made it clear I did not want to speak to him. "It would be rude," was my immediate response. It seemed inconceivable to do such a thing to someone who had been in my life for so many years. Letting it settle into my consciousness that this was indeed an appropriate response changed the landscape for me.

Women may eventually come to the point where they will only accept contact with their partner through an attorney. These decisions are difficult because they are not the normal way of responding to people. It goes against the principles of many women to refuse to speak to someone. It may be awkward to say little beyond hello to him at their children's events. But women have a right to protect themselves, and these limits may be necessary for this protection. Any contact between abuser and survivor may be like offering beer to an alcoholic; it sets in motion an accelerating string of contacts, none of which necessary or healthy.

Sometimes only drastic action is sufficient. Thousands of women flee to shelters every year, forced to abandon their homes and the security of familiar surroundings in order to escape harm. Such desperate measures increase their losses at a terribly difficult time in their lives, but they need to take whatever action is necessary to reach safety.

Protecting themselves from boundary violations is about women taking back their power. As a result of living in an abusive relationship, women have learned to give up power that rightfully belongs to them. As human beings they have a right to hang on to their own legitimate power. They have the right to say no. They have the right to choose the people they will be intimate with in their lives. They have the right to live without fear.

Establishing boundaries includes learning to recognize when a woman's power has been taken away—and figuring out how to take it back. While she was with her partner a woman may have tried to change her life by convincing him to change his. That effort was futile. Thinking she can protect herself by persuading her partner to leave her alone is a continuation of that pattern. She should not be surprised to find out that that effort is also futile.

A woman needs to make the mental shift toward figuring out what *she* can do to change the situation. She can't make him stop calling her house, but she can get an unlisted number. She can't make him stop calling her at work, but she can stop answering the phone. She can't make him stop mailing her letters, but she can stop opening them.

Those choices carry repercussions. An abuser will most likely retaliate when his victim takes back her power, and it is important that she think through how her partner may respond to any course of action. He may retaliate financially or physically. If she simply stops opening mail, she may miss essential information. If she accepts information only through an attorney, her partner may make unnecessary contact just to run up an expensive bill. A

Minnesota man killed his five-year-old daughter and then committed suicide to punish his former wife for trying to set limits on his contact with her and their daughter.

Setting boundaries is not the same as controlling another person, although an abuser will scream that it is. It does involve a transfer of power, which is what he is actually reacting to. When women set boundaries they take their power and return it to where it belongs—in their own hands. When a woman pleads with her partner to leave her alone she is trying to get *him* to change his behavior. When she gets an unlisted phone number, she can let go of his behavior because *she* has found a safe channel of communication between herself and the outside world. He can call anyone in the entire world he wants to—including his children on a separate line—he just can't call her.

Gavin de Becker is a security expert who advises movie stars and major political figures. He is also a survivor of intense childhood abuse. His book, *The Gift of Fear*, is the result of his experience in both settings. De Becker advises all targets of stalking and harassment to avoid responding to the harasser whenever possible.[18] He says:

> *People . . . wrestle with their options, rarely seeing that doing nothing provocative is an option too. . . . There is an almost irresistible urge to do something dramatic in response to threats and harassment, but often, appearing to do nothing is the best plan. Of course, that isn't really doing nothing; it is a reasoned management plan and a communication to the pursuer every bit as clear as direct contact. This approach is a real test of patience and character for victims, but it is often the fastest way to end harassment."[19]*

Abusers enjoy the struggle. They want to elicit fear and anger in their victims. To the extent she responds to him or tries to confront him, his victim reinforces his behavior. Confrontation and reaction are payoffs for him. If at all possible, women should avoid providing a payoff to their abusers.

A woman cannot stop her partner's behavior, but she can choose not to reward it. She can't make it better, but she can avoid making it worse. If she manages to avoid responding to harassment for two months and then confronts, she simply teaches him to keep at it for two months and a day. Although she may not be able to avoid vibrating internally when he makes contact, she can try not to give him the benefit of seeing her fear.

With each incident of harassment she can keep telling herself, "Don't react, don't react, don't react." People who are attacked by a bear sometimes survive by playing dead during the assault. They cannot stop the bear from attacking, but they can make the attack less interesting. Sometimes the bear loses interest and simply walks away. A woman cannot control her partner's behavior, but she can do everything in her power to keep her own energy where it belongs.

Coping with harassment takes courage and persistence. Abusers can be ingenious at developing checkmate situations, where every alternative provides a payoff. Some will suddenly begin attending their children's athletic events, sitting close to their former partners in the stands. These women have the choice of not attending the event, and thus leaving their children unsupported, staying in place and allowing the harasser to be successful in making contact, or moving to another seat and appearing petty and rude to other parents, who may have a friendly relationship with the abuser. Each new situation requires thought and careful action—a process that can be exhausting.

While living with an abuser, many women develop a habit of instigating an incident in order to end the mounting tension. The tension of submitting to harassment without responding can seem unbearable. But any response reinforces the harassment and keeps the victim and her abuser locked in the cycle. The journey toward freedom requires that women learn that they don't have to respond, at least in their behavior, and that they have the capacity to step outside the cycle. The abuser's cycle does not need to determine his victim's behavior. And, eventually, it no longer needs to determine her feelings either.

A woman who avoids unnecessary contact and has learned to discipline herself not to respond to provocation cannot possibly be accused of instigating or even contributing to harassment. And yet incidents continue; incidents that may require complex strategies on the part of the abuser and perhaps the knowing or unknowing cooperation of others.

Strategies that shift the locus of control from the abuser to the survivor include changing locks on a house, hanging up or not picking up the phone, getting an unlisted number, refusing calls at work, not opening mail, not speaking when approached, negotiating only by voice mail, and immediately ending a conversation if it becomes sidetracked.

Many men see a restraining order as a challenge, advises divorce attorney Linda deBeer, and beating the system becomes a game to them. Gavin de Becker cites a study by the San Diego District Attorney's Office that states that approximately half of the women surveyed believe that orders for protection worsened their situation.[20] While restraining orders can be useful, they are not a panacea and can be counterproductive. Each situation needs to be evaluated individually.

A survivor knows her partner better than anyone else. She needs to use that wisdom in developing her strategy to cope with his harassment, although experts can be very helpful in suggesting possible alternatives. Developing a plan will involve thought, guesswork, and a certain amount of trial and error.

Calling the police when an abuser shows up may be an effective deterrent for some, but for other men it may be a payoff. Police departments vary greatly in their response to abuse and harassment. Informal intervention by police seems to be a relatively effective means of slowing down harassers.[21] According to the National Violence Against Women survey, 15 percent of survivors said the stalking stopped after their abuser received a warning from the police, while fewer than 1 percent said stalking stopped as a result of a restraining order. Many abusers are cowards, and while a piece of paper does not intimidate them, confrontation, particularly by a confident man, does. However, many men are very skilled at keeping their harassment beneath legal limits, and so even sympathetic and savvy police departments may not be able to help everyone.

Survivors need to learn to be consistent in their response to harassment. The cycle of abuse teaches many women to respond differently at different times. Particularly as they are transitioning out of a relationship, women may have times when they yearn to return or when their partners seem repentant. Without firm evidence of permanent change, any unnecessary contact between abuser and survivor simply prolongs the misery.

Setting boundaries is not easy, particularly for those women who do not have good boundaries in other areas of their lives. Kip Walker, a pastoral minister in Eden Prairie, Minnesota, advises, "Practice on the easy guys." Women should try saying no to people who are respectful and who genuinely care about them and experience the relief that comes from being honest and direct about what they want and don't want.

Women shouldn't expect the process to be easy when they first start asserting boundaries. The idea was very new to me. As I was learning to set limits with other people in my life, there were times when I couldn't bring myself to confront someone directly—so I left a voice mail message. I was embarrassed to not have the gumption to do things the "right" way. While using voice mail is not as direct as conversation by phone or in person, it's better than not setting the boundary and then acting out discomfort or, worse yet, hiding it. With practice, survivors will become more confident and skilled at being direct.

Setting boundaries uses the power of healthy anger in a positive way. Taking action can help women transform their simmering resentment or impotent rage into an effective anger that passes and leaves them in peace. Setting limits is freeing.

INTERNAL BOUNDARIES

In addition to learning how to maintain physical boundaries, a survivor also needs to develop emotional boundaries. While keeping her abuser at a physical distance is important, her ultimate freedom rests in learning to disconnect the internal buttons that set her heart pounding and her thoughts racing. This can be a slippery process. It is easier to make changes in behavior than in thought processes.

A survivor needs to develop the discipline to redirect her thoughts. When she becomes aware that she is obsessing about her partner, she needs to make a choice to try to focus her thoughts in another direction. At first that shift may last about four seconds. She may feel as though she is redirecting hundreds of times each day and having absolutely no success. But making the effort to distract herself does have an impact, and making the attempt is better than simply letting her thoughts run wild.

One step that is important in establishing internal boundaries—keeping the good in and the bad out—is to consciously direct energy away from bitterness, resentment, or vengeful thoughts. Anger and revenge are contagious. The ultimate defeat would be to allow the abuser to transform the survivor's spirit into one that resembles his own.

Abuse survivors often have serious work to do in learning about and developing boundaries. Books, the advice of professionals, and caring friends can help them become more aware of changes they need to make about boundaries in their lives, both with their former partners and with others. The Appendix provides some guidelines for boundaries for those women who must have ongoing contact with their former partners.

SPIRITUAL BOUNDARIES

I believe there is also a spiritual element to setting healthy boundaries. Trusting a power greater than themselves leads women to freedom in all areas of their life, but particularly when they are the focus of another person's destructive intentions. The oppressive darkness of stalking and abuse can develop an energy that seems to go beyond the purely material reality.

I believe that surrendering myself to God's protection was an important step in finding the strength to maintain my emotional boundaries. While survivors are still suffering intensely from the impact of abuse, such surrender may not make them feel better, but it can still make them *be* better.

Martin Luther King, Jr., once said that he could not possibly have continued his battle for civil rights without a source of spiritual strength. He needed to believe that ultimately the universe was on the side of goodness and that there was meaning within the suffering he witnessed and experienced. Early in his work he became understandably frightened of the death threats made against him and his family, and he questioned whether to continue the struggle. One night, alone at his kitchen table, he had a powerful experience of God's presence. From that point on, his courage and determination never wavered.

Not everyone has one of those extraordinary glimpses of a higher power, but they can put themselves in a receptive frame of mind, open to the reassurance that God gives. Those who belong to a faith community can seek out people who are willing to pray with them for peace and protection. This act of trust does not have to be done within the context of any particular religious tradition. Members of Twelve Step groups such as Codependents Anonymous or Al-Anon often find this strength in their meetings.

Women can privately entrust themselves to the care of God as they understand God, and over time that dedication can contribute to their ability to be at peace with their situation.

Spiritual boundaries and emotional boundaries are closely intertwined. Finding a sense of spiritual protection can give women a sense that there is *some* place that is safe for them, even if that place feels as though it's just a very narrow ledge. Holding on to that safe place and knowing that they are protected there helps them find the strength to set and maintain emotional and physical boundaries.

It also helps to keep the abuser in proper perspective. When a woman gets to the point of being terrified, when her abuser seems to break through every boundary she creates, he can begin to appear larger than life. Contact with a higher power reminds her that her abuser is a child of God—and that no one is ultimately more powerful than God. Even if her abuser were to succeed in taking her life, God would be with her on that journey as well.

MARKING THE MILESTONES

For most survivors, recovery will be a slow process, with relapses and losses as well as gains. There is value in taking time to mark and celebrate victories—the moments when a survivor recognized a boundary issue and stood up for herself. She can celebrate by reading over old journals to review her progress, by treating herself to dinner with a friend, or by creating a symbol to remind her of positive change. Rituals, such as lighting a candle and offering a prayer of thanksgiving, can bless new steps forward. Each victory, large and small, deserves to be noticed and celebrated.

LEARNING DETACHMENT

Learning to detach—to stop trying to control other people—is another component of establishing healthy boundaries.

As a matter of survival, some women tried to control, contain, defuse, manage, and change their partners' abusive behaviors. Some learned this controlling behavior after they became part of an abusive relationship. For many, however, it was ingrained in them long before they met their partners. In any case, it is well established by the time the relationship ends, and it is something survivors need to change if they are going to be free.

Codependents have an unhealthy focus on controlling and reacting to other people's behavior. Generally they are aware of this on some level, if only because their lives aren't working very well. Often, other people try to point out a woman's lack of boundaries to her. She is told to slow down, that she's too nice, that she works too hard, that she spends too much time taking care of other people. Secretly, she may agree with them, but it seems as though she can't help herself. Her lack of boundaries causes her to take on other people's problems as if they were her own. On other days, when stress is getting the better of her, people may complain that she is angry and controlling. A woman's lack of boundaries causes her to try to change people or to punish them when they don't change. Faulty boundaries underlie her compulsive caretaking and the stress it produces.

Some psychologists call this *overfunctioning*. Because their partners *underfunction*, refusing to take responsibility for their own behavior, survivors try to do it for them. Harriet Lerner, Ph.D., defines overfunctioning as "an individual's characteristic style of managing anxiety and navigating relationships under stress." She says overfunctioners:

- *know what's best not only for themselves but for others as well,*
- *move in quickly to advise, fix, rescue, and take over when stress hits,*
- *have difficulty staying out of and allowing others to struggle with their own problems,*

- *avoid worrying about their own personal goals and problems by focusing on others',*
- *have difficulty sharing their own vulnerable, under-functioning side, especially with people who they believe have problems, and*
- *may be labeled as people who are "always reliable" or "always together."*[22]

Many survivors of abuse are guilty on all counts.

Survivors need to realize that part of recovery is being willing to take a look at their own dark side. Compared to an abuser, victims look like saints. But compared to an abuser, most people look like saints. That's not the point.

The point is, compared to whom I am *capable* of being I rarely look like a saint. I have always thought the saying "They were just doing the best they could with what they had" is baloney. I haven't done the best I could since I got up this morning. I haven't done anything terrible, but I haven't done the absolute best I could—it's not human nature to do so. There are days when I do a whole lot less than my best.

The reality is, I do try to control people. I did try to figure out ways to stop my husband from abusing me. And I intervened, appropriately, thousands of times, to interrupt his abuse of our children. I monitored the volume, intensity, and duration of his tirades. I always had an ear cocked, ready to move in. Often I tried to control him because he was hurting someone. Sometimes I tried to control him because he was making me uncomfortable. And sometimes I tried to control him just because I wanted my own way.

There are all kinds of ways survivors try to control people. They may try to control people's perception of them by being nice. They may try to make sure that their children don't reject them by dropping everything when they need something. This is perfectly natural—it's just that codependents tend to take it to extremes.

A major part of every woman's recovery process is dealing with what's called the "locus of control": whether she perceives her life to be controlled by her own will or by that of others. Paradoxically, the process of finding a woman's inner power can include learning to rely on an outside source of power—a higher power. An image I use is of swimming in a stream. The stream is intended to carry me toward its destination. The stream is moving, with or without me. I can struggle desperately to keep my footing, standing against the current and being buffeted by it; I can grab tightly to branches hanging over the banks, trying to resist the movement downstream; or I can trust the current, allowing my feet to be lifted off the bottom of the streambed, swimming safely around boulders on the way. I don't know exactly where the stream is taking me; I cannot see around the curves that lie ahead. Chances are there will be rough patches in the water, but the stream itself is good and wise.

I can trust a wisdom and strength greater than myself, rather than depending on myself to play God and run the world. As I have progressed in my recovery I have become more realistic about my strengths and my limitations. I know that most of life is out of my control, but under God's guidance. And I recognize that the stream is carrying others—including my children and my former husband—on a similar journey.

Although she needs to take action to protect herself or another person, a survivor needs to understand that her abuser will not change until *he* decides he is ready. The likelihood that she can make it happen is extremely low. I know. I tried. I tried being patient. I tried praying. I tried counseling. I tried threats. I tried arguing. I tried pouting. I tried explaining—I was convinced that if I could only explain things clearly enough to him he would surely change. I thought separation and divorce might work— they didn't. And if I think honestly for two minutes, I can see why. I don't like it when someone else tries to take over my life, even if they think it's for my own good. Why should my former husband—or anyone else—respond positively?

Al-Anon advises its members that they "didn't cause, can't control, and can't cure" a loved one's alcoholism. The same holds true for survivors of abuse. They didn't cause their partner's abuse, they can't control it, and they can't cure it. They can decide where they will be in relation to it, and what they are going to do about its effects on them. And they can grow to the point where their lives are about living, not about coping with an abuser's behavior.

Like my former husband, who will always be an abuser, I will always be a codependent. My habits are simply too strong. The real question in my life, as in his, is whether or not I am consciously and actively working on recovery.

One of the humbling and necessary realizations of recovery is just how "hooked" a woman may have become. Recovery requires that she recognize the ways she tries to control and learn to let go of those urges. I have made major progress in this area, but some days I just dress up my attempts to control so they look better. For most survivors, control has become such a part of life that they are like fish that are totally unaware of the water that surrounds them. Like fish, they can learn to leap into the air and discover there is another world.

A survivor's life is filled with hooks—choices she makes repeatedly that do not serve her well. Some hooks, like abuse and alcoholism, are obvious to the world and clearly destructive. Learning to unhook from managing other people can be more difficult because the hook is invisible—at least to her. Often the lack of wisdom in her choices is very apparent to outsiders—she just won't listen to them.

Refraining from trying to control an abuser is not the same thing as ignoring him. Abusers can be dangerous. I am not encouraging anyone to simply ignore an abuser. For some women, failure to pay attention can cost them their life. Survivors need to pay attention, be realistic about risk, take the steps available to protect themselves, and repeat the Serenity Prayer by Reinhold Niebuhr:

God, grant me
the serenity to accept the things I cannot change,
the courage to change the things I can, and
the wisdom to know the difference.

5

Preparing For and Finding Support

Developing healthy boundaries goes hand in hand with reestablishing old relationships with friends and family and learning to make new connections with trustworthy people. When survivors set boundaries with their former partners, they open space in their lives and their hearts for more healthy relationships. As they learn to say "no" effectively, they will discover that they can have a greater degree of safety in the world. The growing security of knowing they can protect their boundaries gives them new courage to selectively let people close and allow them to touch their lives.

Developing a network of healthy, supportive relationships is a process. A first step in beginning the process is for the survivor to come to terms with how alone she has become, and why.

ISOLATION

Isolation is one of the hallmarks of abuse. Abusers isolate their victims in order to increase their own level of power and control. Victims isolate *themselves* out of shame and discouragement over the abuse they are experiencing. Even if they have active lives and many relationships, they often shut friends and family out of the most intimate and frightening part of their days. Their desire for privacy, combined with their partners' efforts to isolate them, leave them feeling lonely and helpless

THE ABUSER'S ROLE

Many men take drastic measures to cut their partners off from outside relationships. Some will follow their partners around, monitor car mileage, open mail, demand an accounting of actions when out, or break off family relationships. Women in rural areas can be particularly vulnerable to this type of isolation. Cutting telephone service and refusing to allow a partner to drive effectively imprisons a woman who lives out of sight of neighbors or passersby.

"Steven" used more subtle strategies to isolate his wife from the outside world. He became annoyed when she talked on the telephone. He was critical of her friends and family. If she went out, she had to call home frequently and felt pressured to return as quickly as possible. She invariably paid for her absence with an argument on an unrelated topic when she returned. Most powerfully, she knew her children suffered while she was away. She was afraid of what might happen if she was not there to intervene. Steven often greeted her return with, "Things didn't go very well while you were gone."

Catching glimpses of the abuser's rage may make friends and family uneasy. A woman may abandon or limit friendships out of fear of what people will encounter on entering their home. Their children's friends may feel anxious in the abuser's presence, creating embarrassment and isolation for the children as well. She may avoid going out in public because she is embarrassed by her partner's behavior while she is with him.

SELF-IMPOSED ISOLATION

In addition to a partner's direct efforts to isolate his victim, abuse carries its own isolation. If a partner is not clearly abusive in public, the victim often carries her secret in silence. She knows her life is very different from the world's perception of her. There is a deep loneliness in not being truly known by anyone. I am always stunned by the smiling family portraits published alongside news stories of women murdered by their partners. Serene public faces often shield terrible tragedy.

Some people may discourage a survivor from telling her story. They may brush her off or downplay an incident she tries to share. Survivors are generally very sensitive to cues from outsiders indicating whether or not there is a willingness to listen and "get" what is going on. When she is ignored or put down, she learns to keep her stories to herself.

"Ilsa's" husband locked her in their bedroom and took the room apart, finally throwing the mattress on top of her and hurling a pillow in her face. When she recounted the incident to their marriage counselor, the counselor laughed with her husband about the incident. When she objected, the counselor assured her that the laughter was not a problem, since the incident would not be repeated. The message was reinforced: Don't bother telling.

Gradually the accumulated secrets lock the victim in a cell, alone. The habit of not telling takes on a life of its own. She feels ashamed to be with a man who behaves in such a fashion. There is an odd sense of shared responsibility, of owning the shame because she is in the same house with the abuse. Over the years I heard about abused women who shared their sadness with no one, and I wondered how they could go through life carrying that silent burden. It was not until after my former husband left home that I realized I had also kept the secret. Not until I began to share my story did I realize just how much I had been holding inside.

Depression, a common result of abuse, carries its own isolation. Depression makes it virtually impossible to *feel* support even if it is being offered. Severe depression may make it impossible for a survivor to go out in public or to church or social events. If people do not understand the reason behind her absence, they may misunderstand it as aloofness or indifference. By the time she finally leaves her relationship, she may have been set up—and set herself up—for almost total isolation.

COPING STRATEGIES THAT DON'T WORK

Some women cope with loneliness by throwing themselves into work, parenting, or activities. They run from their inner lives, burying their pain under outside commitments. Church and volunteer activities, valuable in themselves, can take on an unhealthy importance. They are with people, but in a less than whole way. One night a few years ago I came across a magazine article that stopped me in my tracks. A cynical but pragmatic school administrator was quoted as saying, "If you want something done, ask a middle-aged woman who is unhappy at home." I had no idea I was so obvious. The comment cut deeply, but I felt helpless. I knew I was compulsive about my work, but it provided me some protection from the pain of my marriage.

When she finally separates from her abuser, the full impact of the victim's isolation hits her in the gut. As difficult as her relationship was, at least she still had someone in the house with her. There may be people who care about her, but she has pushed them away, not allowing them to see her or her life in any kind of real way.

TELLING THE STORY

Telling the story of her abuse is a critical part of breaking out of the survivor's aloneness and moving toward recovery. As long as she keeps the abuse a secret she increases her partner's ability to shake her confidence in her sense of reality. Even though she knows his perspective is false, she has heard it so often that she may begin to believe it. This is particularly true if she experienced abuse in her family of origin; her ability to hold on to her own reality was damaged at a very early age. "Stacy" described it: "I feel as though someone put me in the dryer and turned it on. I know which way is up, I just can't keep my body headed in that direction."

This sense of scrambled reality is sometimes called "crazymaking." It's like being locked in a fun house at the circus with mirrors that make people look two feet tall. Survivors need to find real mirrors that reflect themselves and their lives in their true light. The "big lie" theory holds that if you tell a lie often enough and loudly enough, people will eventually believe it. Some women have truly been overpowered by the big lie.

The only way back to wholeness is to be heard and recognized. But a survivor will not be helped by talking to just anyone. The majority of people in the world do not understand what she is experiencing, and many do not *want* to understand. A friend wisely told me, "Stop looking for support in places where you're not going to find it." It is a waste of energy trying to convince people to listen. The fact that someone *should* be willing to understand and be supportive means nothing. Survivors need to find people who in fact *will* understand and be present to them. Her repeated experience of being discounted by her partner makes a dismissive response from others especially demoralizing—but she needs to keep up the search.

For a time the only people that may be willing to listen are those the survivor pays to do so: a therapist or a facilitated support group. If the survivor can't find someone to listen for free, then she needs to pay someone to listen, if she can afford it. She needs to keep looking until she finds someone who understands the dynamics of abuse and will take her seriously.

I recently heard a powerful story of healing that occurred in a Central American village. The village was poverty-stricken, and all able-bodied members went out into the fields each day to work. Older women stayed behind to care for the children. One day an old woman disappeared; she was captured by outsiders and tortured for three months. When she returned to the village she was so overwhelmed she was unable to speak or even care for herself.

Uneducated as they were, the villagers knew that in order for her to heal she needed to be embraced and heard. The villagers decided that each day one person would stay back from the fields to be with her—to hold her and listen to her. Although the community depended on the productivity of each worker, they were determined to bring their comrade back to life. Those who listened to the horror she had endured knew her fate might be theirs at any time, but they persisted in their courage and generosity—and they healed her.

MEETING RESISTANCE

Many survivors will not experience the generosity of those Central American villagers. Separation and divorce make many people uncomfortable. They feel awkward and unsure of what to say. The silence can be deafening.

In addition, many people do not want the security and stability of their lives and communities shaken. A friend's divorce may threaten some couples' sense of safety and they respond by distancing themselves. This rejection may be even more intense if the divorce is a result of something as disquieting as abuse. People want to pretend that everything is fine, in their own marriages and in their circle of friends. Author Paul Kivel calls this the "myth of the happy family."

> *The myth [of the happy family] allows us to attack anyone who speaks out. When someone says, "This arrangement is not working for me because I am being abused, discriminated against, having my land taken away, being denied my freedom," we immediately respond by saying, "You are creating a problem with your complaints. Everything was okay until you brought this up. After all, we're really one big happy family and we care about each other."... Our "families" will always look happy to those with more power, privilege or prestige, and will always be dangerous for those of us with less. A happy family can only exist when justice*

*prevails, and when everyone in the family has an equal and
adequate amount of power, safety, participation and
autonomy.*[23]

People can be brutal in sending the message that survivors
should get over it, shut up, get lost. This rejection and silencing
comes at a time when they are particularly vulnerable, and it can
be devastating. Known as "the bystander effect," the pain of
being abandoned by people who could help and choose not to
can be hard to bear. It is particularly painful when it comes from
people considered to be friends. Survivors would do well to
remember this when sometime in the future they are on the sidelines of someone else's pain. Their deeper understanding can
prompt them to have the courage to offer support to someone
else who is being isolated.

Some abusers will make a concerted effort to infiltrate every area
of a woman's life and win over her family, friends, acquaintances,
and coworkers. This strategy can be absolutely stunning to watch
as she discovers how many people will allow themselves to be
manipulated rather than speaking up. These contacts are an
attempt by her abuser to isolate her from others while maintaining his contact with her.

If a man is successful in doing this, he effectively neutralizes his
victim's story. She may need to leave many dear and familiar
places to find a spot where her voice can be heard and her reality
recognized. The loss of long-term friendships and familiar haunts
is difficult to bear, but it may be necessary. She may need to give
up some of her old supports, which no longer function, to find
new connections that can truly help her. This transition can be
frightening and heartbreaking. The history of her abuser, and her
own personality and temperament, will determine the best course
of action for her.

In order to heal, a woman needs to find her own village. This can
be challenging. She is at a period of her life when she is not always

easy to love. She is messy, she cries, she gets angry, she is hyper-sensitive, she talks too much or too little. Yet within all that she is a child of God who deserves support. Fortunately there are people who are willing to love even the vulnerable and unattractive—and who can love her while she comes back to life.

HELPING PEOPLE LISTEN

As she gets stronger, a survivor will be better able to manage sharing her story. When times were hardest it seemed I was leaking emotions all over. After bottling up so much for so long, I seemed to have lost my ability to contain myself. I reacted intensely to insignificant comments, I shared personal things when I shouldn't have, my resentment would flare up unexpectedly—in short, my pain was overwhelming. I had kept my distress hidden until I was past the breaking point—and then I spilled.

Survivors can learn to help others "contain" the reality they have shared with them. Most people are not accustomed to talking about things like abuse. The subject frightens them because it disrupts the world as they have known it. Yet society needs to acknowledge the existence of abuse in order to tame it. A survivor can help people listen when she learns to disclose appropriately. People are more able to hear her if she is not seething with resentment or vibrating with fear. A select few can hold her when she is in that condition, but the vast majority of people will avoid her and her experience.

The select few who have generously agreed to be on call for her will hear her at her most vulnerable. But normally she needs to share judiciously and in small doses. She can disclose whatever is appropriate at the moment and then consciously return the conversation to a normal tone. People are often caught off guard by the difficult topic and do not know what to do. A common response is to ignore what has been said. Even though she is the one living with the pain, and she would love a quick empathic response, the survivor needs to take the lead in helping people learn to acknowledge such matters.

When I tell people I have written a book about recovering from an abusive relationship, there is often a startled silence. They have learned, or suspect they have learned, something personal and unpleasant about me. They usually are thinking, "Wait a minute, is she talking about herself? What's going on here?" I tend to move the conversation along, to help the other person find a way to navigate out of an awkward moment. It is in my best interests to help them see me as a full person, not simply a survivor. Coworkers and acquaintances need to know they can talk with me on a range of subjects without fear of frequent and unpredictable references to distressing parts of my life.

"Talia" was taken aback by a question from her coworker "Amy." A friend of Amy's was dating Talia's former husband, and Amy had heard at work through the office grapevine about the harassment Talia had experienced. Amy wanted to know if she should be concerned about her friend. Talia was startled at the question but then briefly outlined her history.

This conversation disrupted the normal flow of their workplace interactions. Afterward, it was important for Talia to reestablish a comfortable and appropriate work relationship, one where the primary link was the workplace, not the intimate details of a failed marriage. Even though Amy had initiated the conversation out of concern for her friend, Talia had much more experience in "containing" her history and thus in protecting the environment in her office.

FINDING HUMILITY

A survivor needs to develop humility in this process. Humility is not thinking she is less than other people. Humility is honestly assessing herself and who she is in relation to those around her.

Humility means being willing to acknowledge that she is in need, but also to recognize that other people have needs.

If a survivor is not used to sharing her story, it will take time before she is comfortable asking someone for support. If her pattern has been to complain at every opportunity, she would do well to shift the focus of her conversation. Complaining is very different from asking for support. Complaining sustains the status quo; asking for support seeks additional strength to handle the situation effectively.

Connecting with someone can be important in managing herself, especially in the early stages of recovery. Reaching out to someone and talking for a while can mean the difference between a manageable incident and one that throws her off balance for two weeks.

A survivor should consider developing a list of people to call when fear threatens to overwhelm her. Of course, she should ask their permission first, to see if they are willing to take on this generous task. She also needs to be conscious of the limits of the people on the list. They need to know that they can resign if listening becomes too hard. Even the best-hearted people can become worn out if leaned on too often or too heavily.

Early in recovery she may feel that she is being a burden. Perhaps she is; but there are people in the world who are good enough to shoulder the load. My friend Holly was gracious enough to say that she felt privileged to accompany me on my struggle. Holly's generosity made it easier for me to call on her.

The survivor's turn will come. When she is back on her feet, she will have the opportunity to hold and listen to others who are in pain, whether it be the result of abuse or other loss. For now she needs to admit her weaknesses and rely on the strength of people with the generosity and courage to care for her.

BEING CAUTIOUS

It is important for a survivor to stay safe if she is trying to form connections while still living with her partner. Abusers know that connecting with outside support will translate into greater internal strength for their victims. They may worry about damage to their reputations. Even an abuser who seems not to pay close attention may be very sensitive to anything that has the potential to move his victim toward freedom. There is always some risk attached to freeing herself from the isolation that binds her.

The Internet can be a good source of information and connection, but survivors need to be aware that their partner can trace their "computer tracks" if they connect to the Internet at home. A computer at another location such as a public library may be a safer place to seek information and help. They should learn to clear their tracks from whatever computer they use. Shelters and resource centers can help women balance the risks and rewards of finding support.

LOOKING FOR HELP

An abuse recovery group can be enormously valuable for any survivor, and a quick search on the Internet can help her find one. Women living on farms or in small towns have particular challenges in finding help. Shelters and recovery programs are scarce in small communities, and people have a tendency to know one another's business. Safe access to the Internet, if she can find it, can be especially helpful under those circumstances.

Al-Anon groups are geared to people living with alcoholics, but if she substitutes "abuse" for "alcohol" a survivor can feel right at home in an Al-Anon group. The Internet or a telephone book can give information on nearby groups. Other Twelve Step groups can also be helpful.

Congregations—churches, synagogues, and temples—can provide connection and support even if she does not share her story there. She should avoid hiding out in impersonal groups, like potluck supper committees. Activities that include personal connection, such as a faith-sharing group or scripture study, may give her more opportunity to share her soul with others.

Staying connected to family and building healthier relationships can help her find support and develop inner strength. Healthy family members know her in ways no one else can. By strengthening healthy family relationships, women can rediscover parts of themselves lost in the struggle of surviving abuse.

Survivors should try talking to their friends about both the bad and the good in their lives. They can choose friends who are discreet and will not spread their abuse story throughout the community. But they need to keep in mind that friendships should be as balanced as possible. Even when they are suffering, survivors can give as well as receive support.

FINDING A SPIRITUAL CONNECTION

The challenges of life, and in particular the challenges of abuse, are too great for a woman to handle on her own. She needs love. If she had never received human love in her life she would have trouble even getting up in the morning, let alone taking on recovery. All women have received some measure of human love in their lives, although some people survive on a remarkably small portion.

There is another source of love available to a survivor that is deeper and more profound than the love any imperfect human being can give her. Monotheistic religions like Christianity, Judaism, and Islam speak of this love as a person: a living God who thinks and chooses, who consciously created her and loves her. This God knows her heart intimately and created her out of a vision of who she has the potential to be. This God works with her and the circumstances of her life to help her discover and claim her very deepest and truest self. She can talk to this God, ask him to intervene in her life, and she will be answered.

A HIGHER POWER

Many people today reject the traditional notion of God. Some have been wounded by their experience of church, by hypocrisy, judgment, or even abuse from people affiliated with religion. They are more comfortable speaking of a Higher Power rather than the more traditional notion of God.

The best depiction I know of this Higher Power is the *Star Wars* movies. "The Force" is an unseen source of power, available to anyone who chooses to access it. The Force does not listen or speak, but people who align themselves with it experience power and guidance they cannot achieve on their own.

Another approach is to compare a Higher Power to electricity. Electricity is a powerful source of energy. I cannot see electricity; I can see only its effects. If I knew nothing of electricity, I could be in a room filled with lifesaving medical equipment but unable to use it because I would not know how to turn it on. Electricity's power for good only works if an item is hooked into the electricity, and hooked in properly.

In the same way, the Higher Power is there; it is available, if a person just learns how to use it. In a sense, the Power doesn't "care" about people in the same sense that a personal God, or a friend, does. And yet it sustains them and is a source of love and care. They can enter into the power and direction of the stream, and their lives will be infinitely better if they do.

There are significant differences between a belief in a personal God and in a Higher Power. There are variations in a person's understanding of a Higher Power, as there are variations in a person's understanding of God. Both images hold tremendous power to carry them in the direction of love.

Many people who begin to trust a Higher Power eventually come to name that power God. Many do not. But a life lived in relation with God or a Higher Power is fundamentally different from one that is not. That is not to say that people who are not believers are bad or ignorant, any more than people who have not come across electricity are bad or ignorant. But they encounter the world differently.

The following sections deal with finding a connection with a greater Being. I use the term God here and ask readers to mentally shift to whatever term resonates with their experience.

THE WISDOM OF TWELVE STEP PROGRAMS

I said earlier that survivors' behavior patterns have some of the characteristics of an addiction. They can be hooked on the moments of closeness and caring in their relationships, or they can be hooked on trying to be in control. They might, unfortunately, be hooked on drama. Addictions can be a response to pain in their lives, or they can be a substitute for a sense of meaning or a connection with a power and reality greater than themselves.

Recovery can be facilitated through the core wisdom found in the Twelve Step program. Millions of people have found peace and serenity through Twelve Step recovery groups such as Alcoholics Anonymous and Al-Anon. The hallmark of these groups is surrender to a Power greater than themselves, developing a growing and conscious connection with "God as we understand God," and a conscious and consistent process of learning to clean up their lives.

The language of Alcoholics Anonymous and other Twelve Step recovery programs is very deliberate. People working the program will speak of God, of "God as we understand Him," and of a Higher Power. Many people who join these groups have been wounded by their experiences with institutional religion, or simply have not had a positive experience with organized religion.

They may have been judged for their addictions and even told they were marked for hell. People working "the program" have learned not to allow those experiences to block them from a tremendous resource for recovery. Surrender to God is at the core of Twelve Step recovery and, in fact, of all major religions.

Many women may have survived enormous challenges on the strength of their faith, and this section is simply a reminder of what they already know to be true. Even those whose faith is life-long can become sidetracked by the challenges in their lives and forget to "let go and let God." The key to this is learning to surrender to God.

LEARNING TO SURRENDER

Surrendering is not the same as praying, although it may well involve prayer. Too often when people pray they are simply taking time to inform God of how they think he should handle things. Surrendering is radically different. Surrendering puts things in God's hands and asks, "What do you want me to do?" It is opening up to God's light on the issue.

The chance that a person is right and God is wrong on any given topic is extremely low. The stark logic of this fact somehow does not stop people from acting as though they are the ones with the inside track on best solving a challenge.

The idea of surrender may be a new one for some survivors. They may have no idea how to do so. Trying to teach someone to surrender to God is a bit like trying to show someone how to whistle—the kind that uses two fingers at the corners of the mouth. The problem is, no one can see what's going on in someone else's mouth. The only way to learn to whistle is to watch a demonstration, listen to the explanation, and try over and over until a sound comes out.

Surrendering is similar. Someone explains the benefits of surrendering and how to do it. Then people have to try it for themselves.

There is some skill involved. It's not that God discriminates against people who don't "do it right," just as electricity doesn't discriminate against people who don't plug their hair dryers into the wall. Until people learn how to listen, they can't *hear* what God is saying. And until they learn to let go, they will keep on clutching and getting in the way.

A friend uses an image I find helpful. She described surrendering her children to God's care (mothers are notorious for having difficulty letting go of their children). She envisions her children as rocks. She imagines herself putting each of the rocks out in front of her, placing them on the ground before her, open to God's light. Then—and this is a very important step—she imagines putting her hands behind her back.

When I give a talk and describe this process, listeners usually smile at the thought of putting their hands behind their backs. They trust God—to a point. But they want to hover close, just in case God gets it wrong. They keep their hands just a few inches away, ready to clutch, to take back, to fix. Surrendering means they actually trust that God will provide—that his wisdom and love is greater than their own. They trust God enough to put their hands behind their back.

Surrendering is not the same as passivity. It is the same as being coachable, like a talented athlete who still lets a wise coach guide her. The athlete is out there, working up a sweat. She is making many decisions. But she is watching the sidelines for signals and heads back to the bench for direction at regular intervals.

Sometimes survivors do a better job surrendering other people to God than they do themselves. They can trust that there is love available for other people—but it is harder to trust that they are truly, deeply loved themselves. They need to spend time absorbing that reality. Prayer and meditation give them time to be in God's presence and allow God to touch them. There are people who can shine the truth of God's love into survivors' hearts, and there are ways in which love can come to them only in silence, but God calls them at every moment. They are in God's hands at this very hour.

DISCOVERING A SOURCE OF GUIDANCE

Faith in God opens survivors to a source of love that is unavailable elsewhere. It also provides them with guidance. So often they are called to make decisions where the outcome is hidden from them. Deciding whether or not to leave a relationship, deciding on a strategy to respond to harassment, making a decision about a child, choosing to risk another relationship—they cannot know the outcome of those choices. It is rare for God to give an absolutely clear direction on the path to take, but God often leaves hints. Learning to read those hints takes time, and it takes wisdom to recognize when their egos or desires are getting in the way of the message.

Relying on God's guidance and connecting with other people who do provide survivors with a level of safety they cannot find elsewhere. The older I get, the more I believe that the success of relationships depends largely on the rules people play by. There are certain rules—strategies for expressing themselves, standards of respect—that protect people and relationships. Understood properly, a relationship with God raises these standards of behavior.

On a bad day, when I am stressed and not inclined toward generosity, I may have trouble coming up with a reason why I should be tolerant. But remembering that everyone, including my former husband, is a child of God is nonnegotiable. When I try to see a person in the same light God sees him, my vision shifts.

This is not to say that nonbelievers are not respectful or moral people. There is nothing more courageous or generous than a person who has no belief in God or the afterlife but sacrifices his life for another. When my standards of respect and love rest on something greater than myself or my own limited resources at any given moment, I am more consistently able to honor those standards.

6

Healing the Damage

The trauma of abuse takes a tremendous toll on the survivor's humanity. I begin this chapter with humility and a certain hesitancy. Millions of women worldwide are repeatedly beaten and raped by their partner each year. An astounding number of women endure this treatment throughout their lives. I am in awe of those who survive to become wise and strong women who care for their children and their world.

Doctor Judith Herman has worked for years with survivors of war, domestic abuse, and incest. Her wise and compassionate book, *Trauma and Recovery*, sheds light on the survivor's unraveling. She says:

> *When neither resistance nor escape is possible, the human system of self-defense becomes overwhelmed and disorganized. Each component of the ordinary response to danger, having lost its utility, tends to persist in an altered and exaggerated state long after the actual danger is over. Traumatic events produce profound and lasting changes in physiological arousal, emotion, cognition and memory. Moreover, traumatic events may sever these normally integrated functions from one another. . . . She may find herself in a state of constant vigilance and irritability without knowing why. Traumatic symptoms have a tendency to become disconnected from their source and take on a life of their own.*[24]

When I attended my first domestic abuse recovery group meeting, I felt foolish describing myself as an abuse survivor. My former husband did not beat or sexually assault me, and other women in the room had endured abuse much more brutal than my own. Yet, after twenty-two years of marriage, I had broken down. Two years before we separated, I reached the point where I could no longer endure the unpredictable and unreasonable conflict. After our marriage ended and the emotional toll of my former husband's harassment mounted, I began to question whether I would survive at all. I spent six full years on the brink, battling with all my strength to hold on to life and myself.

An abuser invariably blames his victim for his actions and tells her she is crazy. He may be able to convince other people that there is something wrong with her. She is not crazy, although she may sometimes resort to crazy behavior. She has been injured by abuse, sometimes to the point of near-total destruction.

Anyone who has been the target of sustained and intense emotional abuse has symptoms, just as anyone who is beat up physically bleeds and suffers physical injury. I am not less of a person because my arm is broken; I am not less of a person because I am depressed or anxious. In either case I am a human being in need of healing.

Sorting out the spiritual, physical, and emotional injuries resulting from abuse is an important step in moving toward healing. Since so few people around her understand the impact of trauma, much of the responsibility for guiding the survivor's recovery is her own.

UNDERSTANDING THE SYMPTOMS OF ABUSE TRAUMA

Mental health professionals who do not understand partner abuse misdiagnose a survivor's experience. If someone were to judge me based solely on my mental health history, they would not be impressed. I have a fat mental health file. Like many other survivors who seek professional help, I have been diagnosed with depression and anxiety disorders. Over the years, therapists have jotted down a variety of mental health codes in their notes. One intake worker informed me, after a single forty-five minute session, that I had a genetic predisposition to depression and medication was the answer. That piece of misinformation is stored forever on some central computer data bank, accessible to any potential future employer or health insurance company.

Sometimes survivors are tempted to judge themselves based on their symptoms—they cry too much, worry too much, are touchy, have headaches and backaches, can't sleep, and have a variety of other physical and emotional ailments. They *have* symptoms—they *are not* the symptoms. They can recover from the symptoms. As intense as these emotions may be, they are not part of their souls. Their souls exist in the choices they make around their emotions. Recovery asks them to sort through the rubble and retrieve the scattered parts of their souls and bring them back to wholeness.

Most survivors of abuse share the following symptoms. Understanding their causes and how they can be treated gives survivors the power to move through and out of them.

ANXIETY

I suffered from anxiety for twenty years of my marriage. Mothers worry about their children, and I would have been a worried mother even if I were not married to an abusive man. I loved my children fiercely from the time they were born, and if anything had ever happened to them, particularly as a result of a mistake on my part, I would have been devastated. So I worried.

But my anxiety had another powerful source. My feelings about trying to live with and manage my former husband's abusive behavior had nowhere to go. I was not afraid he would seriously hurt me physically, or that he would intentionally do serious physical harm to our children. But when they were small I was afraid he might unintentionally injure them while enraged, and I knew they suffered emotionally from his outbursts.

As a mother I felt a responsibility to contain my former husband's anger and limit the emotional damage he inflicted on our children. I diverted his rage from them onto myself and stayed in thousands of conversations because I knew if I tried to leave he would escalate and frighten them more. The helplessness and terror they and I experienced as a result of his rages had nowhere to go. Although I defended them and myself the best I could, there was always residual damage.

My sense of entrapment translated into a generalized anxiety that made me feel as though I were crazy. This anxiety did not have a specific focus but rather came to permeate my view of the world. I worried obsessively about my children. I woke up in the middle of the night terrified of nameless threats. I had recurring nightmares about an assortment of enemies.

I annoyed my children and my former husband and embarrassed myself. I didn't engage in bizarre behavior; I just worried. I felt I might as well walk around with a sign saying "neurotic" pasted to my forehead. When I felt major depression closing in on me as well, I finally told my former husband that I was ready for a divorce. Although we did not separate for two more years, I woke up one morning two months after that conversation and realized that my free-floating anxiety had disappeared. It was not genetic, it did not require medication, it did not come from my concerns about my parenting, it was not a legacy from my family of origin. Anxiety was what I did with my tension about trying to manage my husband's behavior.

Anxiety and fear that is out of proportion to events may well be displaced from a survivor's struggles with her partner. Anxiety is a normal response to unpredictable, ongoing, and frightening events. Generalized anxiety weaves itself throughout a survivor's world, creating a sense of a fearful environment wherever she goes. Some survivors develop phobias—intense and unreasonable fears of specific objects or actions, such as a fear of public places or of spiders. Still others suffer disabling panic attacks. All of these are extremely uncomfortable and may be embarrassing—but they are not crazy.

The internal freedom of knowing I was ready to take action was enough to dispel the miserable fear I had endured for twenty years. It was not even necessary for me to actually escape the abuse for the irrational anxiety to subside. Until that time I did not make the connection between anxiety and my marriage. Although events in my children's lives occasionally trigger relapses that last a few days and subside spontaneously, my generalized anxiety has not returned for eight years, and I do not expect to feel it again. Fear and anxiety are symptoms that something is wrong; they are not innate to a survivor's character and they can be healed.

DEPRESSION

After anxiety came depression, which was more than enough to disable me. I had known for a long time I was nearing a crisis. I had approached it a dozen years before and was somehow able to pull out of the nosedive. My goal was to keep the family intact until my youngest child left home, but I simply did not have the strength.

I knew something was happening to me that was outside of my self. The part of me that was breaking down seemed separate from my soul, as if my body were being overcome by an overwhelming illness. Thinking differently, praying, getting counseling—all the things I had tried to do to cope—were no longer enough to get me through. I had experienced depression before and knew what it felt like. This was not just a matter of saddness getting worse; it was qualitatively a new and devastating condition. So I went to a psychiatrist for an evaluation. She informed me I was in imminent danger of a major depressive breakdown. I took her warning seriously but still did not feel I was free to leave the marriage.

I did not feel like I was crazy; I felt like I was broken. It was like having mononucleosis—my mind was intact, my thinking was basically clear, but I simply could no longer carry on the struggle. I saw myself trying to run across a desert carrying a bucket of water to my children. They needed me to be there for them, to support them, to intervene with my former husband when necessary, to love them and discipline them. I desperately wanted to carry that bucket, but I had become exhausted and dehydrated, collapsed and helpless in the sand. It seemed my only way out was to abandon what I saw as my children's best interests by breaking up my family—something I was unwilling to do.

When I could gather enough strength, I would get up and stagger forward, only to collapse again. I would go to work, clean the house, try to carry on normal conversations. Then conflict would arise and I could feel all strength and energy drain out of me.

I spent two years in this condition. I had been afraid prior to the breakdown—afraid of the pain, afraid I would be unable to come back. It was worse than I could ever have imagined it to be. The very day my former husband finally moved out, the depression began to lift. I remember sitting on the porch that evening, listening to Frank Sinatra songs I remembered from childhood, savoring the peace in the air. I could breathe.

I knew my recovery depended on being able to stay clear from my husband, and I naively thought the divorce would provide that protection. Like so many other women, separation simply began yet another rocky stretch of the journey.

POST-TRAUMATIC STRESS DISORDER

My former husband's harassment precipitated yet another challenge for me: Post-traumatic stress disorder. Post-traumatic stress disorder (PTSD) is a common condition among survivors of abuse. The current technical definition requires that a person experience a real or perceived threat to her physical life, such as attempted murder or a natural disaster. Abuse threatens the soul. My fear was that I would survive physically, but that terror, anxiety, and resentment would so dominate my life that I would cease to be myself. The thought of being alive but losing myself was far more frightening than the thought of physical death.

The suicide rate for PTSD is alarming. One of the hallmarks of PTSD is that it does not respond well to traditional forms of treatment and often gets worse over time. The constant state of tension eventually takes on a life of its own and disables women. I considered suicide in spite of my love for my children and my faith in God. I was desperate.

HYPERVIGILANCE

Because her emotions are intense and the harassment unpredictable, a survivor may suffer from something called hypervigilance: an excessively alert state in which she constantly scans the horizon for traces of her partner or his actions. This vigilance can be intensified during harassment. When she lived with an abuser, she at least knew where to find him. He wouldn't climb in a window in the middle of the night to attack her—he didn't need to because he came home every evening for dinner. Harassers delight in taking their victims by surprise. Being contacted in settings she thought were safe, and that may have been safe in the past, can escalate her fear to new levels.

While she was in the relationship she maintained some illusion of control. Leaving the relationship was an attempt to gain appropriate control over her life—to protect herself from the hostile intrusion of abuse. Discovering how little control she has over harassment can trigger hypervigilance even among women who have escaped its effects throughout their relationship. A feeling of reasonable control over her life is essential to a basic sense of human security.

My unrealistic fears evaporated, but my terror of my former husband consumed me. After a few years of harassment he was always on my mind. When I was teaching classes, a part of me watched the door, fearing he would enter. Walking the halls between classes, I was afraid he might suddenly show up. At the grocery store or in a mall, I was terrified I would encounter him. He lived in my neighborhood, our children attended the school where I taught, and for a year and a half he dated a parent of a student there. My expectation of encountering him was realistic, but my response to those encounters was not.

Eventually I dreamed of men attacking my children and me all night, every night. I could not sleep for more than two hours at a time. I thought about leaving the state, but to do so would have meant leaving my life—my children and my work.

SHOCK AND CONFUSION

Abuse can break down a survivor's ability to think clearly. The "fight or flight" response—reactions humans and animals share on a physical level—has a third response: to freeze. Both humans and animals are known, under certain circumstances, to become almost hypnotized by their attacker. They go blank and become compliant. They cannot think, and they do what the attacker demands or seems to expect of them. A more primitive, emotional, and reactive part of the brain takes over, and the ability to think clearly is overcome. Research indicates women experience this stunned effect much more frequently than men.

When I first consulted Laura, my therapist, it was as if I was in a form of shock. I could carry on basic daily activities but I had lost my ability to process information around my former husband's abuse. My early sessions with Laura were humbling. She would talk to me and at the time I would understand the literal English meaning of her words but I was unable to comprehend what she *meant*. This inability to *really think* contributes to a survivor's vulnerability. She can be helpless in an encounter because she literally cannot think of what to do. This sense of paralysis contributes to her despair of ever being able to find herself again.

RUMINATION

A woman who has experienced abuse has suffered trauma. Rumination is a classic response to trauma: mentally obsessing over what her partner has done, what he might be about to do, or how to respond to either. After years of abuse, a relatively minor incident can bring out a major response from her. It's like the childhood torture some little boys enjoy of punching a buddy repeatedly in the shoulder. The injured area becomes more and more sensitive until eventually the slightest touch resonates throughout the body. Rumination is a survivor's ineffective attempt to shield her emotional bruises from the next punch.

When her partner acts out she has a tendency to continuously replay the incident. She rehearses what she might have said that would stop the incident from happening. She runs the conversation through her mind over and over again until she is sick of herself—and then she runs through it again. People tell her to forget about it, to let go, but she can't.

The brain accommodates stressful information by temporarily storing the memory and then going back to reprocess the incident. To see this dynamic in action, consider a dog that narrowly escapes being hit by a falling ladder. After running away, the dog will approach the ladder timidly at first, sniffing the air, poised and ready to flee if it should start behaving strangely again. He will approach and retreat, checking for safety. Each time he comes a little closer, until finally he has investigated the ladder thoroughly and assured himself that the world is once again normal and safe.

When an abusive incident occurs, a survivor tries to take it apart, check out each piece, and then somehow fit it into her understanding of her world in a way that makes sense to her. She tried to reduce the power of the incident by understanding it. With an abuser, the world is never safe. So she keeps circling the ladder, unable to take her attention away because it has come to life and attacked her so often. Eventually the ladder could move every six months—her abuser might contact her only as often—and her attention would still be riveted.

INSOMNIA

Insomnia is a symptom common to abuse survivors. Insomnia is exhausting and fatigue makes it hard to think clearly. As fatigue accumulates, a survivor can gradually become accustomed to living in what constitutes an altered state of consciousness.

Lack of sleep also contributes to her accumulated stress. Sleep not only refreshes her physically, but also she processes information while she sleeps. Memory is affected by lack of sleep, and REM sleep, or the deep sleep of dreaming, is an important vehicle for processing emotion. REM sleep occurs in the later stages of the night—a stage of sleep an insomniac rarely encounters. When unable to sleep normally for extended periods of time, she accumulates unprocessed data in her nervous system. Insomnia is not only a symptom of but also a contributor to her distress.

NUMBNESS, MEMORY LOSS, AND DISSOCIATION

A survivor's body and soul can only take so much damage. At some point a protective mechanism kicks in and she becomes numb. She gets accustomed to pain that at first would have been intolerable. One way of numbing herself can be to forget—and the good is often forgotten with the bad. For several of my most difficult years I was unable to remember much about my children growing up or to get in touch with the deep feelings of love and protectiveness for them that had kept me going. That loss was one of the most difficult for me to forgive. Recovering those memories and those emotions has been one of the greatest rewards of the healing process.

A survivor may suppress parts of herself in order to protect them. She builds a wall, blocking her memories or desires. During especially difficult incidents, she may put herself mentally in another place: on the ceiling overlooking the scene or in a closet. Such *dissociation* is an understandable attempt to make herself safe. When she begins recovery, she may discover parts of herself that she put away and that seem not to have aged. She may be forty-five chronologically, but her sexual self is still twenty-two, for example. These parts of herself are not separate personalities; they are facets of her being that will need special care and protection when they first return to her.

Assessing the Damage

All of these symptoms are the result of abuse and indicate its severity. Taking stock of the damage is one of the first steps toward recovery. Many domestic abuse counselors begin work with a client by taking an abuse inventory. The inventory maps out the types of abusive behavior she has experienced, their frequency, and their level of intensity. This serves as an assessment tool for the counselor and a reality check for the survivor.

Even a woman who is fairly clear on the abuse in the relationship can find the inventory sobering. She experiences abuse one day at a time, one incident at a time. She tries to cope with one argument at a time, one outburst at a time. The impact accumulates, but she may find it simply impossible to remember every single event. It is not useful to remember everything. But taking a look at the final tally is a shock. Writing down the types of abusive behavior and the number of times she has experienced them over the years is eye-opening. It is like getting the final bill at the grocery store and realizing that all those two-dollar items have added up to cost a bundle.

THE IMPACT OF PHYSICAL VIOLENCE

While a survivor does not consciously remember each incident of abuse, each is stored in her brain. In one of my first sessions with Laura, she emphasized the impact of even one physically violent incident. She reminded me that people, like animals, imprint strongly on traumatic incidents. Even one violent event is stored in the brain and colors every future time the survivor feels threatened by her partner. The most violent incident leaves a permanent mark on those who experience or witness it. Women who have experienced intense physical violence sustain enormous damage to their sense of safety and predictability in the world.

SEXUAL TRAUMA

Very little is said about the impact of sexual trauma in abusive relationships. It may be the very darkest side of partner abuse, and one that takes great courage to mention. One woman I met told of being raped by her husband and her last child was a result of that assault. Rape is horribly traumatic, perhaps even more so when done by an intimate partner.

In addition to cases of clear sexual assault, the very nature of the sexual relationship between men and women puts women at risk. Sexual intercourse can be used as a weapon by men because of differences in anatomy and emotional responses to sex. There are many ways a sexual relationship can be used to intimidate a woman and exert power over her. Simply expecting or demanding sex without regard for a woman's preferences is abusive. Many women have difficulty asserting themselves and saying no and so feel as though they are being raped even though there is no physical or even verbal struggle. Unwanted sex, even if it is not overtly forced, is distressing. Enduring years of unwanted sex is deeply traumatic.

Abusive men are unlikely to be self-disciplined or generous when making love. The sensitivity required to do the "dance" of skilled lovemaking is usually absent. Men may be simply out of touch with the delicacy of women's bodies and cause unintended pain that they do not discipline themselves to avoid.

Arguments over sex can be deeply wounding. Abusers often behave as though a woman's body belongs to him and not to her. The denial women practice in other areas of their life carries over into the sexual relationship. They may deny doing something while in the very act of doing it. Sex is likely to be impersonal. But a married woman generally feels that her husband has a right to some kind of sexual relationship, even if she no longer desires physical intimacy. She may feel she has no right to decline sex, or she may fear the pain of the conversation that follows rejection.

Some abusive relationships have a passionate sexual side that fuels a drive to stay together. Many do not, or passion that existed early in the marriage dies. Simply having to sleep in the same bed with an abuser reinforces a woman's sense of vulnerability. Knowing that at any time during the night a partner can reach over makes her feel unsafe even while she is asleep.

For many women, sexual trauma is a secret they do not reveal even when they finally find help for the other areas of their life. Some survivors lock up that part of themselves forever. By sealing off their awareness of their bodies to protect themselves from pain, they lose touch with themselves as sexual human beings.

IDENTIFYING CORE TRAUMA

It can be helpful for a survivor to identify her core trauma. The core trauma is the area that needs the most careful attention in healing. Depending on her partner's behavior and her own personality, this will be different for different women. For some it might be physical assault, for others the sexual relationship, for still others it may be public humiliation or humiliation in front of the children. Incidents that may hold tremendous power for one woman may be navigable for another.

For "Analisa," her husband's abuse of their children was a source of enormous grief. Their sexual relationship was very traumatic. The physical incidents were unnerving. But the core trauma was being required to participate for hours in arguments that made absolutely no sense.

> *Many of our arguments began over Luis' treatment of our children. He would say or do something ugly to them, and I would object or he would see something on my face. Then it would all start. He would deny that he had been angry, that my little girl had been frightened, or that he had raised his voice. He would say he wanted to handle things differently but didn't know how. If I suggested something, he said I was being controlling and critical, and that I had no right to say I was right and he was wrong. When I said he was hurting the children, he would tell me I had no respect for his opinion. This would go on for hours and hours. He just enjoyed the fight.*

"Luis" got his satisfaction from indulging in rage and denial for hours on end, requiring Analisa to stay actively engaged in the conversation no matter what the cost in terms of other commitments or physical and emotional fatigue.

As a survivor moves away from an abusive relationship, she would do well to find ways to protect herself from similar incidents. Her core trauma did not happen accidentally. Her partner knew what he was doing and will work hard to re-create the trauma even after she ends the relationship. Becoming aware of her greatest vulnerability can help her focus her energy on protecting that which is most vital to her.

HEALING THE BRAIN

The full impact of trauma on a survivor's body, mind, and soul is just now being revealed. Wise people have known forever that pain and fear are damaging, but only recently have scientists and psychologists begun to discover precisely how physical, emotional, and spiritual traumas impact the brain and nervous system. This rapidly developing body of knowledge offers new hope to survivors. Options for healing will continue to evolve. Some current healing methods are:

- medication,
- brain-based therapies, and
- guided imagery.

MEDICATION

Medication is often recommended to survivors, and for many it is necessary. Medication can help treat anxiety and depression, although it is not particularly effective for PTSD. It can help overcome the insomnia that becomes a vicious cycle. However, noted expert Judith Herman cautions that medication can be overused, masking the real problem and cutting the survivor off from information important to her recovery.[25]

Some people have a genetic predisposition to depression or anxiety. Their bodies do not produce the appropriate level of chemicals to properly regulate their mood. Medication may be necessary for them on a lifelong basis. For others, repeated prolonged experience has caused their body chemistry to get out of whack, and medication can be a temporary solution while they get back on their feet. In midlife, hormonal changes can affect women's moods and make them more vulnerable to the challenges of living with abuse. Hormone replacement therapy may help stabilize their emotions.

I would never advise someone else on whether or not to take medication; that is a decision for each woman and her therapist. My unprofessional opinion is that, in many cases, there are preferable alternatives to medication that should be tried first. A number of people encouraged me to go on antidepressants, but I was convinced medication was not the answer for me.

Brain-Based Therapies

A number of therapies focus on the neurological effects of trauma. While many survivors have benefited from their use, some are still considered experimental. A few therapies are developing a solid track record with good research to back them up.

A skilled therapist may draw on a variety of techniques to bring about healing. Individual and group therapy can be invaluable, but not everyone has access to them. Some of the alternative methods can be self-administered, but while it is extremely valuable to a survivor to learn new ways to care for herself, abuse carries enough impact that working with a therapist is the safest route, at least in the beginning. Trauma recovery therapy is still in the early stages of development, and unskilled intervention can do more harm than good.

Thought Field Therapy (TFT) and Emotional Freedom Technique (EFT) integrate principles of acupuncture and the body's meridian systems to provide relief. They provide alternatives to more traditional therapy. Both techniques have their advocates and their opponents, and they are still being researched.

The Thought Field Therapy Training Center of La Jolla, California, explains that TFT "gives immediate relief for PTSD, addictions, phobias, fears, and anxieties by directly treating the blockage in the energy flow created by a disturbing thought pattern. It virtually eliminates any negative feeling previously associated with a thought."[26] EFT is a psychological acupressure technique that uses the same pressure points as traditional acupuncture, but without the needles.

For over a year Laura, my therapist, encouraged me to try something called Eye Movement Desensitization and Reprocessing (EMDR). Her description of the technique sounded flaky, and I didn't believe it would work, but when I finally reached the point of desperation I agreed to give it a try. EMDR is a deceptively simple therapy. The basic procedure is as follows.

A therapist asks her client to call up an image: a recent event, a long-ago memory, a recurring fear, or even a dream. The client identifies the emotions she has around the incident and where those emotions are held in her body. She also identifies an unhelpful belief about herself that accompanies this image, such as "I am powerless," or "I am unlovable," or "I will never be happy."

Then the client focuses on the image while the therapist slowly moves an object back and forth in front of the client's eyes. Some therapists use another form of stimulation to trigger the process. The purpose is to alternately stimulate the right and left sides of the brain while being present to the distressing emotions and core beliefs that are causing the client trouble. There is no change in consciousness as in hypnosis, although research indicates a shift in brain waves.

The client, with the support of the therapist, directs the process. EMDR should never be attempted without the aid of a properly trained professional. It is possible to surface memories or reactions that overwhelm a client, and only a well-trained therapist is competent to guide her safely through such an incident.

GUIDED IMAGERY

Guided imagery is a technique that can simultaneously touch a survivor neurologically, spiritually, and emotionally. Belleruth Naparstek, author of *Invisible Heroes: Survivors of Trauma and How They Heal*, is one famous proponent of this method. Naparstek has extensive experience working with survivors of a variety of traumas, and her approach to guided imagery is well researched and carefully developed.

Guided imagery has been described as a form of focused daydreaming. Done with commercially prepared tapes, CDs, or the survivor's recorded voice, she listens to a guided meditation geared toward healing. Calming music often accompanies the narrative.

Guided imagery sidesteps the logical, analytical processes that have been damaged by a survivor's experiences. It appeals directly to the more emotional right hemisphere of her brain, which has been hypersensitized by trauma. Guided imagery can calm the body's overreactive arousal system while helping to replace her distorted thought processes with more soothing, realistic ways of thinking about her life.

SPIRITUAL HEALING

Some women survive their experience through the power of a faith that never wavers. Their sense of God's love and presence remains with them through their darkest days, giving them the resilience they need to face each tomorrow.

For many, abuse challenges their sense of a God who cares for them and who brings meaning and order to the universe. For women who did not grow up with a faith, abuse may confirm their conviction that life is random, governed purely by human choice. Others who have a strong trust in God may find that their convictions sag under the weight of their ongoing pain.

People come to terms with suffering in different ways. Some see everything as part of a master plan set out in advance. To them, everything happens for a reason, and they come to peace with their pain by trusting that someone or something holds that reason. To me, the essence of evil is to go against God's intention, which is love. Everyone has freedom of choice, and unfortunately people often choose less than love. Sometimes they choose against love. I do not believe that God intends or wants people to turn their backs on love or one another.

God can bring good things out of incredible destruction. God does not intend for abusers to harm other people. He doesn't intend for the survivor to suffer from the hatred of others, or for innocent children to be harmed by what they witness and experience. I do not believe God intended whatever wounding in her upbringing that may have impaired a woman's ability to recognize or protect herself from abuse, but God can bring miracles out of those circumstances.

As a Christian, I believe that God is with the survivor in the midst of her greatest suffering. God is not only by her side, but also God took her suffering upon himself—God in the flesh experienced rejection, betrayal, beatings, humiliation, abandonment. God knows the loneliness and bewilderment she feels, as well as the sense of utter defeat. He leads her through the darkest moments on to resurrection.

Many women have felt abandoned by God. They may have prayed diligently, asking God to change their partners' heart, asking for relief from their pain and their children's pain. They may have asked for permission to leave their marriage. Yet in many ways God has remained silent. He may have provided other sources of comfort for them, but their partners did not change. And if they have left their relationship, the pain and loss of that decision is not eliminated by faith. Depression may cause them to feel abandoned by everyone in their lives, including God.

Yet God remains. The image I use is of a father whose child must go through surgery. The father loves his child but is unable to be with her through the surgery. The father not only cannot prevent the surgery, but he also has to give permission for the surgery to take place. God loves his children and is with them, but his presence is often invisible, just as the child is unable to see her father waiting and weeping down the hall. God does not abandon his children, just as a loving parent does not abandon a child even when she is out of sight and out of reach.

Martin Luther King, Jr., spoke of the value of redemptive suffering—undeserved distress that is not simply endured but can transform the sufferer and those around her. One of the painful aspects of the survivor's experience is the sense that so much of what she has gone through is futile. In some sense, coming to terms with abuse includes recognizing the profound waste of time and energy involved in coping with abuse and trying hopelessly to change an abuser. At the same time, suffering does not need to be wasted. So often, a survivor is unwilling to come to wisdom until her unproductive habits are so incredibly painful that she drops them from sheer exhaustion. Many spiritual traditions teach that there is a transforming power in suffering.

I heard Mother Teresa speak many years ago. She said, "The tragedy in the world is not that there is so much suffering. The tragedy is that so much suffering is wasted." Survivors have surely suffered. Their children, if they have them, have suffered. That suffering can leave them embittered and resentful. Or it can make them luminous. Some of the most remarkable people in the world are people who have suffered intensely.

That is not to say that people should go out looking for suffering. Some survivors have that tendency, and it is a betrayal of their deepest selves. But suffering is inevitable in this life, and for whatever reason survivors have had more than their share. It behooves them to learn from it.

Seen in a spiritual light, suffering has meaning that goes deep beneath the surface. Prayer, particularly prayer with others, is invaluable. Praying with others can have a special power to heal the spiritual damage, the sense of abandonment, and the loss of meaning that can accompany abuse.

Recovery is many-faceted, and each woman's journey is unique. Healing takes time, and over the years a survivor may find help from many different sources. The resilience of the human spirit is incredible. She can come back from places she thought were hopeless. She can find joy and serenity again.

Healing gives her strength for another portion of the journey: grieving. Until she heals, she is hampered in her ability to move through her pain. Mourning and learning to forgive hold the power to move her into a new world.

Part Three

Moving Forward

I believe a primary reason women return to a partner in spite of overwhelming abuse is the failure to mourn and accept their losses. Those women who become involved in a series of abusive relationships are somehow trying to avoid losses in ways that are doomed to failure. They can only truly move on to the next stage of their lives by letting go of their investment and their hopes in the relationship and finding new ways to take care of themselves.

Mourning is the hard work involved in processing our grief at losing a relationship and a world we once treasured. Mourning the end of an abusive relationship is especially difficult because our feelings about our partner are so mixed. We need time and the wisdom of others experienced in grief work to help us through this long and challenging process.

In chapter 7 you will work to come to terms with your past and the losses involved in ending your relationship. We can only let go of our losses if we are conscious of what they are. We need to be able to experience all the conflicting emotions involved. This chapter provides support and guidance for being truly present to all aspects of our relationship so that we can get ready to bid it goodbye.

Chapter 8 provides guidance for truly letting go. These pages guide you through the process of actually letting go of your old relationship with your partner and the old world that is so familiar to you. You will begin the process of developing a new relationship with your partner, and begin to discover who you can be without him.

Chapter 9 will help you find peace through forgiveness. Resentment and anger tie us to our old relationship with our partner. As unfair as it seems, forgiveness is a gift to ourselves and to the abuser. This spiritual process is the final step of breaking free from the bonds that limit our potential for living joyfully through the next stage of our lives.

7

Preparing to Say Good-bye

Survivors cannot free themselves from their relationship with the abuser until they grieve and let go of their losses. Mourning requires them to embrace a whole new world of pain at a time when they already feel battered and overwhelmed. Yet they really have only three choices:

- they can deny the pain and allow their lives to be driven by flight from it,
- they can become mired in it and be condemned to a lifetime of sadness, or
- they can enter and move through it.

There really is no other alternative. The fact that a survivor does not want to be in this situation makes no difference at all. The injustice of having to struggle once again is irrelevant. This is where she is.

Fortunately, survivors do not have to leap into the work. They can allow themselves time to go through the process. It will wait for them—for as long as they live. They can choose not to face it, they can bury it below the level of their awareness—but it will not go away.

It's possible to do the work in pieces, as survivors can bear it. In fact, people have been given an internal mechanism that moderates the pain and protects them from experiencing all of it at once. The mechanism is not foolproof, and sometimes even goes haywire, but it is designed to pace their grief work and help them work through it successfully.

Anyone who has experienced a significant loss—divorce, the death of a loved one, or a serious illness or disability—knows that society does not respond well to grief. Many people do not understand the process of mourning and are frightened by it. They let a survivor know, directly or indirectly, that she is expected to act cheerful and not bother them with her problems. Mourning the end of an abusive relationship is particularly complicated and confusing, which makes finding support even more difficult. A good road map for the journey can be tremendously helpful.

Psychologist Therese Rando has worked for more than twenty years helping people cope with death and chronic illnesses. Her book, *The Treatment of Complicated Mourning*, provides wise and compassionate advice on dealing with death. The process she describes for mourning the death of a loved one can also be applied to mourning the end of a relationship. This mourning process has been adapted to provide the framework for this chapter and the two that follow.

There is a difference between grief and mourning. *Grief* is an emotion people feel as a result of loss; *mourning* is the process people must go through in order to move through their grief. *Complicated mourning* occurs when people become stuck or derailed in this process. Complications occur for a variety of reasons, including the person's past history, the circumstances surrounding the loss, and the absence of appropriate outside support. Mourning becomes complicated when for some reason or another people try to

> *(a) deny, repress, or avoid aspects of the loss, its pain, and the full realization of its implications and (b) to hold on to and avoid relinquishing the lost loved one.*[27]

Mourning an abusive relationship is bound to be complicated. The contradictions involved in an abusive relationship, the fallout that occurs in other parts of the survivor's world, and the damage she has sustained as a result of abuse all complicate the picture. But that does not mean the situation is hopeless. It does mean that grieving will require further attention, more time, and greater wisdom. The gift of mourning is that it also has the potential to heal. Contemporary losses in a survivor's life call up previous losses from her past. For example, a woman who was abandoned by her father as a child will be even more intensely affected if her husband abandons her and their children. The presence of these earlier losses increases the level of pain around her current losses—but it also makes those earlier wounds available for healing. If she embraces the opportunity in spite of the pain, she can move toward greater freedom than she has ever enjoyed. She can become capable of loving more fully in all her relationships.

Women need to be aware that mourning of any kind is more complex than most people realize and requires much more time than they expect. While it can be discouraging to view the long road ahead, it is affirming on the days when they seem to be making little progress. Most survivors find themselves struggling well beyond the date when they thought they would be "over this," and certainly beyond when most other people expect them to be over it. The prevailing myth is that one year is sufficient time to grieve major losses. In reality, several years are usually required. This is a tribute to—and cost of—the love women hold for important people in their lives. Breaking the process down into understandable and manageable pieces helps them be patient with themselves as they continue to move forward—one day at a time.

The Treatment of Complicated Mourning identifies six steps in the mourning process and describes the tasks needed to accomplish each step. These steps fit equally well with a survivor's experience of mourning the end of her relationship. In general, the steps build on one another, although in real life mourners often move back and forth among them. Failure to complete one step will generally interfere with final resolution of a later step.

Mourning happens unevenly. Grief comes in waves. Some mourning simply happens naturally. Other grief work is triggered by events: signing divorce papers, moving from a home, spending holidays without the children. It is all painful. When survivors learn to use it to move forward, it is all valuable.

MOVING THROUGH THE PROCESS OF MOURNING

STEP ONE: RECOGNIZE THE LOSS

Recognizing the loss has two components: *acknowledging the loss* and *understanding the loss.*[28]

ACKNOWLEDGING THE LOSS

Admitting that the relationship is over appears to be easy. However, in addition to the natural human tendency to try to shield herself from pain, there are two factors that can get in the way of the survivor's ability to acknowledge the end of the relationship. One is the cycle of abuse. She may have despaired of her relationship many times, only to be convinced by her partner to come back, or she may have talked herself into going back against her better judgment. This repeated experience of false ending makes the real ending much more difficult to internalize when it finally comes.

The other obstacle results from the escalation of abuse that almost invariably occurs when women leave. She may have expected to have some sort of relationship with her former spouse after divorce. She thinks she knows the degree of loss she is choosing. However, the harassment that often follows separation makes it unwise for her to have any unnecessary contact with her former partner. The increased hostility also reveals that the person she thought she knew either never existed or has disappeared.

The loss is more profound than if her partner had died; a loss that becomes apparent only gradually and requires ongoing adjustment and response.

Understanding the Loss

Comprehending why the relationship is over is also difficult. As much as she's seen of her partner's patterns, it is still hard to understand why he makes the choices he does. Although abusers follow their own internal reasoning, their behavior defies logic from an outsider's viewpoint. It is incomprehensible why an abuser chooses not to recover once the proper tools are available. It is bewildering to watch someone throw away everything he says he wants—a loving family, a relationship with his partner—in order to hang on to behavior that is so clearly counterproductive. But in spite of her inability to understand an abuser's decisions, a survivor needs to understand the full implications of the end of the relationship.

Step Two: React to the Separation

There are three sections to reacting to the separation, all of which are tough. They are: *experience the pain; feel, identify, accept, and give some form of expression to all the psychological reactions to the loss; and identify and mourn secondary losses.*[29]

Experience the Pain

No one likes to be in pain, but pain has the essential function of letting a woman know that something is going on that needs her attention. Ending a relationship with someone she loves or has loved hurts terribly. She may have learned to run away from pain. She may run toward it for some reason and get tangled up in it. Healthy mourning requires her to walk through pain slowly enough to let it touch her but quickly enough that she is not overtaken by it. She needs to do this on both an emotional and an intellectual level; if she simply *thinks* about her experience, without letting herself enter into it, she will not be able to progress.

FEEL, IDENTIFY, ACCEPT, AND GIVE SOME FORM OF EXPRESSION TO ALL THE PSYCHOLOGICAL REACTIONS TO THE LOSS

Reaction to loss can take a variety of forms. Grief and sadness are the most obvious, but a lesser known reaction is guilt, and it can be paralyzing. Some women feel torn by guilt for leaving the relationship, others for staying as long as they did, and some for both. Sorting through the decisions the survivor made, understanding her own limitations and the scarcity of options available to her, and having compassion for herself can help her move through guilt.

Anger is another emotion people use to shield themselves from pain. It is normal to be angry with an abuser; it is tempting to get stuck in anger and resentment. A survivor can also become stuck in anger at those around her who may not react as she would like. Getting beneath anger and resentment to the underlying hurt is part of the mourning process and can ultimately open the door to forgiveness.

IDENTIFY AND MOURN SECONDARY LOSSES

Secondary losses can be aspects of the survivor's loss that are not immediately apparent or that occur as a result of the end of the relationship. Identifying and breaking down these losses is an important part of making grief work manageable. It takes time, patience, and fortitude. If she is unable to sort out secondary losses, a single event can trigger the grief of all her losses. Visiting a place she once enjoyed with her former partner calls up her pain at being alone, the impact of the abuse, and her sense of financial vulnerability—all jumbled together. Hard things are more manageable when taken on one at a time. Each woman's secondary losses are unique. Some of the possibilities are:

She grieves the end of her dreams. She looks at photographs taken at the beginning of her relationship, the two of them smiling and looking confidently into the camera. They dreamed of a loving, stable, long-lasting relationship. They dreamed of being a couple forever, of enjoying friends and growing old together. If they had children, she remembers their dreams of being good parents together, of being grandparents together. So many dreams now lie trampled in the dust at her feet.

She grieves the loss of her innocence. Abuse has changed her. Even if she experienced abuse in past family or romantic relationships, she thought this relationship would be different. She grieves the abuse she took because she thought he loved her, and the innocence that caused her to trust in that love. She grieves for the young woman she was, who did not know such a thing could happen to her. She grieves that she now looks at men, other relationships, and her future with new, more skeptical eyes.

She grieves the end of hope. She survived and stayed with her husband in the hope that somehow things would get better. As clear as it was to her that her loved one was not changing today, there was always the hope that tomorrow would be different. She harbored the hope that she could somehow fix it—that even if it didn't get better tomorrow, it might next week. But when the end of the relationship comes, there are no tomorrows, no more opportunities to make it right. There is no future with the whole family under the same roof. Grieving and letting go of this hope is one of the most difficult tasks she has. It is *essential* if she is to find the strength not to go back.

She grieves the loss of her partner's good qualities. She grieves his sense of humor, or his smile, or his love of music. She grieves the intimacy she had or thought she had. She grieves the loss of the unique qualities that make up the essence of another human being, qualities that perhaps no one else may see in him. Or, conversely, she may grieve that another woman now is enjoying what endeared her partner to her. She grieves the love she has or had for him, and the fact that she can no longer express that love.

She grieves the role her partner played in her life. She may grieve the loss of a husband or a daily partner in parenting. She grieves not having someone to advise her on the small decisions of daily life. She grieves not having a companion when she goes to parties or family functions. She may grieve the loneliness of bearing the burden of car and home maintenance alone. She grieves no longer being part of the "couples world."

She grieves the loss of her illusions about the relationship. Discovering the true nature of her husband's feelings toward her is a shattering new level of loss. Before the end of the relationship, she thought she understood him. She knew his behavior was abusive, but she was mistaken in her belief that he wanted to be different. When it came down to the wire, he refused all opportunities to really change.

Not only is the aggression now more obvious than before, but also the fundamental lack of love gradually becomes apparent, deepening the loss beyond anything she would have imagined. She comes to realize that the hostility and lack of love were probably there from the beginning.

She grieves the lack of closure. Unless an abuser decides to recover, the survivor will never be able to directly say good-bye to him or the relationship. Closure is terribly important when dealing with the loss of a loved one; it is why communities expend so much effort and take so many risks to retrieve bodies lost at sea or in war or natural disasters.

She has imagined the conversation where she explains how she feels to her partner and he finally, *really* acknowledges the damage and says he's sorry. She needs to grieve and let go of the expectation that her partner will ever truly take responsibility for what he has done. She needs to devise another way of saying good-bye and finding closure in her relationship. This lack of closure is particularly difficult if there are children and the relationship is therefore ongoing and abusive.

She grieves that her children will never have a father who maturely loves them. A few men who abuse their partners are loving and caring with their children. Most are not. The anger, sense of entitlement, and lack of empathy that make partner abuse possible make healthy parenting unlikely. Women are often shocked and dismayed by their husband's treatment of their children after divorce.

Some men abandon their children when divorce occurs. Others court the children, trying to monopolize their time or even align them against their mother in retaliation for her leaving the relationship.

Many men reenter their children's lives once the hard work of parenting is over. Abusers tend to see their children as peers. When children are young, their fathers resent the attention the children get from their mother, punishing them and her for providing the care her children need. Much of the abuse directed at children springs from this lack of maturity. When children come into adulthood, men may come to see them as enjoyable social companions.

A woman looks at her children, at the priceless human beings they are and how much she loves them, and in her heart she is sure their father must some day recognize the treasures he has been given. She needs to come to terms with the abuser's limitations as a parent as well as a partner.

She grieves the damage to her children. While she is still with her partner there is the hope that things will change and she can reverse the damage she knows is being done to her children. She remembers their vulnerable faces when they were little and regrets the fear and pain they have experienced at the hands of their father. She regrets the pain she has caused them as well—anger that spilled over from her own misery, and anger that was simply a result of her own shortcomings. She regrets the times she failed to give them the nurturing they needed because her attention was diverted to trying to manage her marriage. She instinctively wants to protect her children from pain, particularly from pain that is inflicted intentionally. The end of her relationship, and the events that follow it call forth her grief at their distress.

She grieves the loss of years that cannot be reclaimed. She has a new understanding of the lament, "I gave him the best years of my life." She will never again be the young woman who began the relationship. If she stayed for many years she will never again be a young mother, cherishing those early, innocent years with her children. While her life has not been wasted, she will never win back those years or have the opportunity to spend them in a more joyful way.

She grieves the loss of her memories. Some divorced couples maintain a friendship with their former spouses, but this is impossible with a nonrecovering abuser. The severance of relationship that is necessary with a harassing abuser cuts her off from many of her memories. There are so many moments in her children's lives and in her own past that she has forgotten but would remember if she were to hear the story told. Her husband may tell stories—but rarely in her presence. There are memories of their early days together, of herself as a younger woman, of him as a younger man. Those memories are important to her, and many of them are lost because she has no one to remember them with.

She grieves the loss of a man in her life. A survivor fears she will never find another mate. That fear is realistic, particularly for mature women. There is a myth that really healthy people are perfectly content being alone, and if she yearns for a partner there is something wrong with her. That myth puts further pressure on her. Human beings are created for love. She can adjust to life as a single person, and life can be good as a single person, but there is an ongoing sense of loss when she lives without a partner. That loneliness provides the impetus for her to continue her search for intimacy in her life; when she is unsuccessful, it hurts.

After divorce, a woman loses not just her husband but also her couple friendships. Over time she may be able to reconnect with the women in her circle of friends, but she may no longer be invited to parties or social events. She misses being in a social circle of both men and women. She misses the relaxation and safety she took for granted as a married woman. She misses walking to her car without fear after an evening event, comfortable because she did not walk alone.

She grieves the loss of an exclusive relationship. If her partner was faithful while they were together, that fidelity was important to her. It was a compensation she needed to cope with the turbulence in the relationship. But when the relationship ended, her partner was legitimately free to start a new relationship elsewhere.

She may be totally unprepared for her reaction when her former partner finds someone else. After many years together, the knowledge can be agonizing. It feels like the final betrayal of the promises made to each other so many years before.

She left him because he chose to not change. She left because the abuse was destroying her and the children. She is alone, often raising her children on her own. Their sexual relationship may have been traumatic; she felt violated in that most intimate part of herself. And now he is with someone else.

Many abusive men's fidelity to their relationship is very shallow. Frequently, men are looking elsewhere before their feet are even out the door. Many women are shocked to discover how truly limited their partner's commitment has been. Often men will harass and try to control a former partner while actively pursuing other relationships for themselves.

When her partner becomes involved with someone else, he may bring another woman to places that are or have been intimate between the two of them. For example, her children's important events have been, or should have been, moments shared between parents. She needs to grieve the loss of those moments as purely "theirs" and accept that someone whose presence is painful for her may well share them. Those moments are some of the most significant and difficult times when she learns in her heart that the relationship is truly over.

She may grieve the loss of her place in the community. Divorce is remarkably disruptive. Not only does it tear apart families, but it also impacts extended families, friendships, congregations, and community networks. Some people form opinions and take sides. Some people fear divorce may be contagious and abandon both parties. Extended families can be disrupted. In-laws may cut off contact.

Couples who were seen as having it all together are suddenly humbled, and each individually may have difficulty developing a new role in the community. A woman who is forced to move out of her home may need to start over in a new community.

She may grieve not being believed. Many women keep the abuse secret until the end. She does not tell for a variety of reasons, but in her heart she hopes that if she *does* tell her story it will be believed. She at least thinks people who love her—family and friends—will believe her. Many of them do. Some may not, at least at first. Many abusers are relaxed and engaging in public, therefore outsiders may find it difficult to believe what a survivor says about her abuser. Some men will confess their abuse in such a way that people are convinced he must be exaggerating—such a sincere guy could never *really* do the things he describes.

Even their children can be fooled. There is no doubt in their minds about their father's abusiveness while he lives at home. However, their desire to have a loving father may be so intense that they will move into denial when they are no longer confronted by daily evidence of the abuse. There is a bewildering sense of injustice when the truth is discounted and, by extension, a survivor and her suffering are dismissed. Her helplessness in the face of disbelief adds to her partner's power and is one more source of grief.

Every woman's losses are different. Every woman processes those losses differently. Recognizing losses, naming them, and sorting them out helps her to deal with her pain in manageable portions. This takes time and emotional energy. She needs to be compassionate and patient with herself, and find others who will do the same for her.

STEP THREE: RECOLLECT AND REEXPERIENCE THE LOVED ONE AND THE RELATIONSHIP[30]

Recollecting and reexperiencing her partner and her relationship requires that she (a) *review and remember realistically* and (b) *revive and reexperience the feelings.*[31] In other words, a survivor needs to allow herself to be present to the whole of the relationship, both intellectually and emotionally. This is particularly challenging when grieving an abusive relationship because it is so difficult to reconcile the positive and negative parts of the relationship. The isolation that frequently accompanies abuse and the love/hate relationship it commonly produces predispose her to trouble in this part of grieving.

Very often a survivor feels an intense sense of relief when she first separates from her partner. At first she may have no feeling of loss, but there are very real losses when the relationship ends. The man she loves is not a monster, or she would not have become involved with him. He holds goodness within him. Being able to feel and work through her sadness about this loss is important. If the abuser begins harassment at this point, fear and resentment may block out any positive emotions she might have about her partner. Remembering the good times or allowing herself to miss her partner makes her vulnerable, and so she pushes those feelings out of her awareness.

On the other hand, a woman may feel only regret and longing after leaving her partner, and feelings about the negative qualities that make ending the relationship necessary become unavailable. While a woman may know intellectually that she needs to leave, the gut awareness she needs to stick to her guns is hard to access. Particularly if her partner is wooing her and pleading with her to come back, it can be hard to remember or really believe the awful things that have happened.

To be able to move through the mourning process, it is necessary not only to recognize intellectually but also to reexperience the positive *and* the negative emotions. It is normal to have trouble integrating these two sides of the relationship. For some women, positive memories may return only after fear has subsided, which can take considerable time. It may not be possible ever to really integrate the two parts of the relationship, but to move forward she needs to learn to be *present* to both of them.

Even though a survivor *needs* to reminisce while mourning, she may be afraid of feeling her attachment to the good parts of the relationship because she is afraid of weakening in her resolve to walk away. When she remembers the good things, the power of the abuse can seem to fade. This period, when a woman struggles to be present simultaneously to both the positive and negative parts of the relationship, can be very risky to the recovery process.

Grieving and letting go of an abusive relationship is more difficult for a survivor than if her partner had actually died. If her husband had died she would probably have had little trouble remembering the good and the bad times. She would have been able to go back and recall feelings of nostalgia, regret, sadness, anger, humor, and joy. The good memories would have remained intact. Instead, she may be numb for an extended time and she may be unable to remember, let alone feel, the good times. When she can remember them, it is hard to determine if they were in fact real, if her partner ever had any real love for her. It is as if death is occurring retroactively before her eyes, progressively blotting out stretches of her past that have helped shape the person she is today.

As difficult as they may be, working through these steps brings the survivor truly present to her relationship in all its complexity. That presence prepares her for the final steps: letting go and forgiving.

8

Letting Go

This chapter provides guidance and support for the painful process of saying good-bye to the life a survivor may have worked hard to maintain. Through letting go, she can open the door to a new life, a new world, and a new identity.

STEP FOUR: RELINQUISH THE OLD ATTACHMENTS TO THE LOVED ONE AND THE OLD ASSUMPTIVE WORLD[32]

This step leads the survivor into the hard and painful work of letting go. In chapter 7 the survivor clarified and named the many losses she mourns. She put things out on the table where she can see them, but she doesn't want to spend the rest of her life simply staring at that table. She *gets* to let go gradually of the bad things in her relationship. She *needs* to let go gradually of many things that are precious in order to be able to get up from the table and move on with her life.

Relinquishing the old attachments to the loved one. Truly letting go of these losses is enormously difficult. As long as she holds on she has hope, however unrealistic, that things will somehow change. Letting go means coming to terms with the fact that her former partner is *not* going to change. She will *never* have a happy relationship with him; she will never have a happy, unified family; she is not going to continue to try to make these things happen. She is dropping the hands she has kept outstretched toward him, and for the moment at least, those hands are empty.

If he had died, there would have been a funeral: family and friends would gather, a eulogy would be given, and the group would go to the cemetery and share a meal afterward. Hearing stories, seeing photographs and symbols of the loved one's life, watching the casket lowered into the ground—all these experiences would help her absorb the reality that there will be no return. If she fell into disbelief over the death of her loved one, she would remember those moments and the reality would be confirmed. Those rituals would have an important role in helping her grasp the truth.

Unfortunately, there are no funerals for relationships that end. Friends and family who know about the abuse often don't understand the survivor's grief, saying, "Why would you be sad about leaving someone like him?" They are unable to help her with this part of her recovery.

It can be helpful for her to find a concrete way of saying good-bye to her relationship and her former partner's role in her life. Some recovery programs encourage women to write a letter to former partners. Writing a letter, speaking in the first person to her abuser, seems to somehow make her words more real. Some therapists suggest reading the letter to an empty chair, preferably in the presence of the therapist or a support group who act as witnesses to the truth of what is being said. Although the letter is a valuable tool for *her*, it would be unwise for a survivor to ever send such a letter to a nonrecovering abuser.

Some women cannot even begin work on such a letter for years after ending a relationship. As bizarre as it may seem, addressing an empty chair may be too terrifying. Emotions may be too raw and unfinished to be able to be put down on paper. She needs to wait until she is ready to write the letter, as writing it prematurely will reduce its power. When she is finally ready, the words may emerge quickly.

Part of the challenge in saying good-bye is reconciling the split between the positive and negative sides of an abuser. Most people are a blend of strengths and weaknesses, but the "Jekyll and Hyde" quality of abusers' personalities resists a coherent response from the survivor. I do not know if I will ever be able to mentally integrate the positive and negative sides of my husband. I solved the dilemma by writing four separate letters. My first letter said good-bye to the parts of my husband and our relationship I cherished. It began:

> *Dear _____ ,*
> *It's over.*
> *Good-bye to you, the father of my children, who was there*
> *with me when they were born.*
> *Good-bye to your special sense of humor that could catch me*
> *off guard and cheer me up.*
> *Good-bye to the freedom to have a friendly conversation*
> *with you.*
> *Good-bye to the young man you were when we were married. . . .*

A survivor clings to the hope that somehow, magically, her former partner will change and his promises will be kept. Until she recognizes and accepts the fact that some of her cherished dreams will *never* be realized, she cannot truly walk away from her relationship. And until she walks away, she cannot begin another, more realistic quest to fulfill new dreams. Another letter I wrote said good-bye to dreams I had and acknowledged that with the end of my marriage those dreams might never be fulfilled.

This letter begins:

> *Good-bye, perhaps forever, to the dream of . . .*
> *Having a man in my life that truly loves me.*
> *Having someone to talk with at the end of each day.*
> *Having a lifelong relationship, someone who shares my life*
> *from youth to old age. . . .*

All people bring negative as well as positive qualities to a relationship. A survivor should never allow a focus on her partner's abuse to provide her with an excuse to gloss over her own failings. Another letter I wrote expresses regrets about my own behavior.

I'm sorry for my self-righteousness, that reduced you to your actions, that sometimes lost sight of you as a child of God and your own unique self.

I'm sorry for being such a terrible housekeeper, and the chaos that created.

I'm sorry for my compulsive overactivity that tangled you up in projects you didn't want. . . .

My final letter is a list of complaints—those losses that resulted from the choices my former husband made to abuse me and our children and ultimately broke our family apart. This letter names the abusive behavior that had such a powerful impact on our family. Naming the behavior puts an end to whatever level of denial I carried and brings my experience into the light of day where it can be healed.

I want you to know the pain you cause with:
the unpredictable eruptions that kept us always on edge,
so many dinners eaten in silence,
the loneliness of living with a husband who never really saw me. . . .

I do not know how to put those four lists together emotionally. Ideally, when a survivor mourns someone she is able to integrate the various parts of his personality and her relationship with him. The walls of denial that protect an abuser from full awareness of his emotions and choices separate the positive and negative aspects of his personality in such a way that she cannot experience them simultaneously. These letters help her name the different aspects of her relationship so she can at least touch them as she works toward the next step of processing her grief.

Relinquishing the attachment to the old assumptive world. Serious loss is traumatic because it shakes up the survivor's perception, not only of the person she has lost but also of the world around her. It is clear, at least theoretically, that she needs to let go of her old relationship with her partner. What is less clear is her need to let go of what is called the "assumptive world." The assumptive world is all those things she assumed to be true but which either never were true or are no longer valid.

Some assumptions she may need to let go of are:
- that her relationship with her partner will continue
- that she will not alone to fend for herself financially
- that if people knew about the abuse they would help her
- that the abuse will not exceed a given level if her partner truly loves her
- that she can protect her children from the effects of the abuse
- that she has to stay
- that abuse happens only to "other people."

It is a relief to let go of some assumptions. For example, a belief that she does not have a right to protect herself sets the survivor up for all kinds of negative experiences. Discovering that she can survive financially gives her new freedom in making independent financial decisions and perhaps in finding new job options. Other assumptions form an important element in her sense of security and place in the world. Relinquishing them is painful and difficult.

Each woman's assumptive world is unique, and the revisions she will be required to make in her new situation will also be specific to her. Many of her assumptions will become apparent only when she bumps up against the reality of a changed world. Identifying and letting go of invalid assumptions is the only means of clearing the way to a new, more healthy and practical way of living in the world. Letting go of her assumptive world may be as difficult for the survivor as letting go of the relationship itself.

STEP FIVE: READJUST TO MOVE ADAPTIVELY INTO THE NEW WORLD WITHOUT FORGETTING THE OLD

To move into the new world, the survivor must:
- revise her assumptive world,

- develop a new relationship with her former partner,
- adopt new ways of being in the world, and
- form a new identity.

Revising her assumptive world. It is natural for a survivor to resist change. As painful and traumatic as it may have been, that world is familiar. At this stage of recovery she is in transition—one foot in a violently rocking rowboat, the other barely on a dock. She needs to climb out of the boat and walk down the dock to dry land, but from her wobbly position the land looks very far away.

It may take a lot of repeated experiences for her assumptions to shift.[33] She needs to go many different places alone before the information travels from her head to her guts that she is indeed a single woman—and she will be okay. She may need to have many sessions with a recovery group before she really comes to grips with the fact that she belongs to that membership—she is a woman who has survived an abusive marriage, and she needs all the outside help she can get to make it through. As difficult as her experiences may be, they are the means by which she becomes willing to revise her assumptions until they more closely match reality.

Developing a new relationship with her former partner. When someone dies, those left behind struggle to take in the loss and then gradually develop physical or mental spaces to enter and connect with their loved one. When my father died my family left his apartment untouched for three months. We then came together and slowly went through his belongings, each of us choosing special items that reminded us of him. His canoe paddles stand in the corner of my living room, reminding me of his love of nature and the friends who shared it with him.

Grief counselors refer to this as "dosing"—gradually being exposed to places and things that remind those left behind of their loved one. Normally, over time they can develop a new, symbolic relationship with the one they have lost. They can draw comfort and wisdom from their memories, even if the relationship was difficult.

An abuser will not hold still for this process. He is alive and often is intent on moving in and out of the survivor's life according to his preferences, not hers. For a time, trying to have any kind of relationship may be even more dangerous and/or more painful than it was before she left. Yet she needs to come to terms with him, if only within her own mind and heart. She needs to develop a new pattern of behavior with him and a new way of thinking about him. This will take time as she develops her own internal resources and discovers the new parameters of his behavior toward her. Those parameters may change on an ongoing basis, causing her to revise her relationship repeatedly over the years.

Adopting new ways of being in the world. A survivor needs to develop new skills and new ways of being in the world. She may need to learn how to maintain cars, handle finances, and negotiate with repair persons or landlords. She needs to learn what it means to be single again. She may need to learn how to date—perhaps in a world that has changed drastically since she last visited. She needs to define herself as an individual, not just in relation to a partner. She needs to adjust her parenting, depending on custody arrangements and her children's relationship with their father. She may need to move to another community or find another job. If the abuse was hidden and became public when the relationship ended, she needs to learn how to carry herself in situations where people's perceptions of her have changed dramatically, for better or for worse.

One of the goals of harassment is to hamper the survivor in moving into a new world. A man may harass his victim in order to stop her from being able to move on with her life. The goal is to punish, but also to distract her—to prevent her from having the time and emotional energy to build a new life. Even a man who no longer wants to actually be in a relationship with a former partner often still wants to own her.

Forming a new identity. Many survivors struggle with identifying themselves as a middle-aged single woman. Society devalues aging, and it does not support single people. Few young people dream of the day when they will be middle-aged and single. There are plenty of young people who plan to stay single, but they intend to stay *young* and single. They may know middle-aged single women they admire, but they rarely hope to actually *be* them. As feisty and beautiful as the heroines of *First Wives Club* were, they all knew they had been left behind. None of them were in a position of their own choosing.

The process of building a positive new identity takes time, attitude adjustment, and experience. The survivor may know theoretically that she has chosen a better place, but she needs experience to actually *show* that her world has improved.

Her partner cannot stop her from moving forward; she simply moves more slowly than a woman going through a more amicable divorce. It will take more time and persistence for her to actually enjoy the benefits of her new freedom. Depression and anxiety can hinder the process of forming a new identity and being successful in her new tasks, but with proper support she can make it.

Step Six: Reinvest in the World and in Relationships

The final step in mourning the end of a relationship is reinvesting in the world and in relationships. Whether or not a woman finds another life partner, there are good places to spend her self and her energy. There are people who need and welcome her love and the gifts she has to share. There are people willing to love her and walk with her. There is good work to do, opportunities to help other people, time to discover and develop talents, and children, if she has them, to care for. She may have struggled through times when it was hard to really believe these things held value. They do. This is where she will find the joy of living. This is where she will find the way out of the pain.

RISK FACTORS FOR GETTING
STUCK IN THE MOURNING PROCESS

Several factors can cause mourning to get sidetracked or derailed. Understanding these risk factors and acknowledging their presence in her life can help the survivor work her way through them. At this point her task may seem monumental; she wonders how she can find the energy even to begin. It *is* a big job, and it will take time. She needs to be patient with herself when progress is slow and be kind and gentle enough to do the work gradually. Clarity about the size and complexity of the task can actually be a cause for hope. Just because she has been working a long time does not mean she is not making headway; it just means she is on a long road. There is sunlight peeking out on the other side of the hill.

Letting go is more difficult when the loss seems preventable.[34] Most women would stay if their partners chose to recover, but they will not. Questions haunt them. "Why won't he listen to reason?" "Why is he willing to throw everything away?" "Why did he decide to abuse in the first place?" "Why did I stay?"

A survivor needs to accept that this outcome was *not* inevitable, but it *is* necessary for her now. She needs to resist the thought that she could somehow have prevented the deterioration of the relationship. Hanging on to this belief will keep her caught up in fantasies and actions that are counterproductive. Her relationship ended because of abuse. She decided the damage outweighed the benefits of staying in a primary relationship with her partner. *She could not prevent the relationship from being destroyed, but the destruction itself was necessary.*

Letting go is particularly challenging when the survivor has other losses, stresses, and mental health issues. People are more likely to get stuck when a relationship is ambivalent, angry, or dependent.[35]

By definition, an abusive relationship has these characteristics. The survivor's relationship has cost her much over the years, so much that she could not possibly have processed it all. She may also have experienced abuse in her family of origin or in other relationships. These previous losses make mourning the end of her relationship more intense, but she *can* heal that earlier pain as she mourns.

Processing her losses is more challenging when she is distracted and her energy sapped by coping with additional factors. Navigating the legal and financial aspects of divorce, running a household alone, coping with harassment, and adjusting to being single all add to her stress. Parenting is challenging under the best of circumstances, and single-parenting her children who are navigating divorce and abuse carries added weight.

Many women do not leave a relationship until depression and anxiety have taken a serious toll on their well-being. These conditions can be overcome, but they will slow the survivor's progress. Their presence will require greater determination in moving through her grief.

Letting go can be difficult because of a lack of social support.[36] Finding good support can be difficult. The survivor's pain and anger can make other people uncomfortable. In the early stages of recovery she may need to receive more than she is able to give. She needs to relearn how to connect with people and ask for help. Asking for help may be humbling and unfamiliar to her.

People who would visit her daily if she had cancer may avoid her if the survivor speaks of her pain. Many good people simply are unwilling to be present to the darkness of abuse. Even sympathetic friends and family are limited in their ability to support her. People who have not experienced abuse simply cannot understand her life. They may have compassion for her and be willing to learn, but much of her experience is simply outside their comprehension. Abuse recovery groups and Twelve Step groups can provide vital support.

Some women need to move out of their homes for financial reasons or to protect their safety. Some need to go into hiding, leaving behind all of their normal means of support. Some are forced to find new jobs, giving up the normal, day-to-day interactions of the workplace that provide their emotional stability. Any of these factors slow down the mourning process and make it more challenging—but they do not make it impossible.

Mourning is a lot like giving birth. It is painful, frightening, and damn hard work. If there were another way to get babies into the world, I'd sign up. Frankly, I can't figure out why God designed labor and delivery the way he did, considering he had other options. But it's the package women are offered—and it is worth the pain.

Through the process of mourning, the survivor gives birth to a new person—herself. Somehow suffering is an integral part of the process. Pain is one of the mechanisms that teach her that her current ways of thinking and behaving are not good for her. I am not at all recommending that a survivor should seek out suffering. Many survivors need to recover from a tendency to seek out painful relationships. Plenty of pain is unproductive; the pain of healthy mourning is not. Accepting the pain in her life, *refusing to inflict it on others*, learning wisdom and compassion, and letting go and moving on all have the capacity to heal not only her own wounds but also those of others.

9

Finding Peace

Many women thought they would find peace when they were no longer living under the same roof with their partner. To be at peace would mean that they could breathe freely, that they could have some sense of security that the next conversation would not blow up in their face, that their mind would be free to embrace each day. Yet many survivors found that they continue to carry the storm forward in their heart. Forgiveness can hold the key to finding the peace they seek.

FORGIVENESS

Forgiveness is a paradox: it holds contradictions that seem impossible to reconcile. Forgiveness is both a burden and a gift. It costs the survivor to forgive another, particularly if that person is not sorry and the injury is great. She resists forgiving people who have injured her. And a survivor who forgives too easily sets herself up to be abused again—an outcome she needs to avoid.

Expecting a survivor to forgive adds insult to injury. Her abuser may have felt entitled to her forgiveness and punished her if she was not prompt in forgetting an incident, but forgiveness is much more difficult and complicated.

Survivors need to remember that forgiveness is also a gift. Many wise people say forgiveness is the only path to true freedom. If they are correct, the only way a survivor can become free is to give her partner a gift he doesn't deserve. Abuse doesn't deserve to be forgiven. But unless she forgives, she will carry bitterness in her heart. Unless she forgives, she will flinch every time she sees her partner, every time she hears his name mentioned, every time she thinks of him.

It is said that we become what we choose. An unforgiving spirit toward her partner contaminates other areas of a survivor's life. The more she chooses to hold on to resentment and bitterness in one relationship, the more easily she moves toward resentment and bitterness in another. It does not matter how terrible the abuse has been; the resentment and bitterness sit in her heart, not her partner's. I do not want to be a resentful, bitter person. The only way I can avoid that is by choosing to forgive.

WHAT FORGIVENESS IS NOT

Sometimes a survivor resists forgiveness because she misunderstands it. Forgiveness is not about failing to hold someone accountable. Forgiveness is not letting someone off the hook. It is not about fudging the score.

It is not saying, "That's okay" or "It doesn't matter." It does matter. It matters a lot. If it didn't matter, she wouldn't need to forgive.

Forgiveness is not telling herself he didn't mean it. Abusers do mean it. Abusers hurt people deliberately, and they hurt people persistently. If a survivor tries to get out of range, an abuser will move heaven and earth to find new opportunities to hurt her. Unless he recovers, he will abuse every woman who enters a relationship with him.

Forgiveness is not saying he couldn't help it. He *can* help it. Abusers may have more difficulty expressing anger appropriately than some others do, but they make very clear choices. If they want to change, resources are available. *Her* recovery requires her to accept that her partner makes choices deliberately. Forgiveness is not a step back from that clarity.

Forgiveness is not giving someone another crack at her. A survivor may fear forgiveness because she has not learned how to compassionately hold her boundaries. She can forgive her partner and still have boundaries. She can forgive him and still leave him. If necessary, she can forgive her partner and choose never to have another conversation with him if those conversations are too dangerous.

Boundaries are not brick walls. They do not need to be protected with guns. They are more like cell walls in the body, designed to keep in the nucleus of the cell and to allow nutrients to come in and toxins to pass out while retaining the cell's integrity. It takes more strength and courage to hold those boundaries without the fuel of anger and resentment, but she can develop that strength.

Anger and Resentment

Anger is one constructive response to hurt. Healthy anger lets the survivor know that there is a problem and gives her extra courage and energy to take it on. In a healthy relationship, she can express her anger and have it addressed, but abusers do not respond to another's anger in a productive way. Her legitimate concerns have not been heard or addressed. Abuse survivors have a reservoir of anger that they have suppressed, turned on themselves or other people, or transformed into resentment or hatred.

Anger is a healthy, normal response to abuse. When threatened, humans are genetically programmed to respond by fighting, fleeing, or freezing. When a survivor is hurt or frightened, anger provides her with energy to protect herself; so she covers her helplessness with anger. When she feels angry the pain of the abuse is dulled; she does not feel disappointment, hurt, or vulnerability so intensely. But the overall toll is greater, because her pain is not processed and so remains with her.

It is impossible to process anger in a healthy way with an abuser. He is not going to listen to her, affirm her feelings, reasonably consider her perceptions, or appropriately come up with a solution. If he would, he would be in recovery. That is not to say abusers are destructive in every instance of conflict. Some are, but many are not. They may sometimes respond well, but the overall pattern of the relationship is negative. In the long run an abuser will discount what she says and feels, punish her for making him uncomfortable, and take care of what he perceives as his own good, no matter the cost to her.

Resentment is anger that has not been expressed effectively and so festers, making her, and those around her, miserable. Among other things, it costs the survivor her power. Used correctly, anger is a useful source of power. Resentment, on the other hand, saps her strength and gives control of her spirit to another. It leaks into other relationships, causing her to react quickly and defensively. Hatred, a total rejection of the other, has the capacity to destroy her and her values.

Unresolved anger is costly. Forgiveness frees her from paying that price.

WHAT FORGIVENESS IS

Then what is forgiveness? It is easier to say what forgiveness is not than to say precisely what it is. Two aspects of forgiveness are letting go of a debt and letting go of anger.

In their book *Boundaries*, Cloud and Townsend say that forgiveness is letting go of a debt that is owed.[37] The survivor's partner owes her a debt. He owes it to her to tell the truth—to himself, to her, and to the people in their lives who have believed his lies. He owes it to her to acknowledge what he has done and offer a true apology. He owes it to her to make amends—to change his behavior toward her in the present, and to try to right the inequities that persist. Without true recovery, he will never pay the debt. It is a waste of energy to hold on to that expectation.

Clutching that debt to her chest, insisting it should be paid, is counterproductive. It's like walking around life carrying a huge rock with an IOU attached to it. She can't pick flowers, she can't hold babies, and she can't run freely, all because her hands are clenched around that rock. Forgiveness is like letting the IOU flutter off in the wind. She sees the signature; she knows it's there. She'll recognize it if she ever sees it again. She just doesn't hold on to it any more. She doesn't allow it to consume her time and attention. Some say forgiveness is letting go of wanting the past to be better than it was. She accepts the reality of her life. She doesn't say it's okay; she simply acknowledges that it *is*.

Some say forgiveness is letting go of the desire for revenge. Many survivors have never desired revenge but have had a very human desire for justice. Forgiveness means letting go of her desire for justice. She is not asked to close her eyes to the fact that injustice has been done but rather to let go of an active, persistent, and hopeless yearning for a just resolution that will never come.

This is why mourning is so important. The survivor is reluctant to let go of something until she has truly grieved its loss. She needs to look long and hard at that IOU before she lets it go. The debt is great. The price she paid for staying in the relationship is enormous. She needs to say good-bye in her heart to *all* the IOU represents before she can completely let it go.

Besides letting go of the debt, forgiveness also means letting go of anger, bitterness, and resentment. Over the years, the survivor may have developed a store of negative memories and emotions, and leaving the relationship does not automatically bring about change. Time does not heal automatically.

A survivor generally carries a greater than average amount of anger because of the thousands of incidents of abuse heaped on her. It is not safe for her to express her anger directly, so she stuffs it, squirts it out sideways, pretends it doesn't exist. With nowhere to go, anger sits inside her and turns to resentment, bitterness, and depression. She may be unaware of just how much anger she carries, but those who love her have probably felt its sting. Forgiveness is a means to letting go of anger, resentment, and hatred, and moving out of depression toward serenity.

TAKING A STEP TOWARD FORGIVENESS

I know I need to forgive my former husband. I want to forgive him—sort of. Even after a lot of effort, I haven't yet totally forgiven him, and I may never do so. Forgiving isn't exactly one of my star qualities. Some people, by temperament or upbringing, forgive more easily. However, I have worked hard at it, and I have made progress. Every bit of progress counts.

The following recommendations have helped me:
- Take baby steps.
- Pray for the partner.
- Pray for God's understanding.

Take baby steps. Author Catherine Marshall speaks of being willing to be willing. The survivor may not be able to honestly say that she is willing to forgive her partner. However, she may be able to bring herself to the point of being *willing* to become willing. She can look at God and say, "I don't see how you could possibly make this happen, but if you can pull it off, it would be okay with me."

Pray for the partner. Jesus taught that Christians should pray for their enemies. This is based on a profound understanding of human nature. God's guidelines are not the result of some external standard that arbitrarily commands certain forms of behavior. God created the survivor and knows how she functions. Jesus' teaching simply lets her know how she functions best. Jesus knows that she reaches healing and freedom through forgiveness. He teaches her to pray for her enemies because prayer gives her the power to turn enemies into brothers and sisters—in her heart.

I learned long ago that praying for someone could be a two-edged sword. If my prayer consists of instructing God on how to change the person, enlighten him, and make him quit being such a jerk, I am simply reinforcing my resentment. In my prayer I am cataloging all my grievances. I am presuming to instruct God, and I delude myself into thinking God is on my side and somehow against the other person. Prayer for change in a person can be appropriate, although the survivor's style of prayer may not always be helpful, but the wrong style of prayer will not move her toward forgiveness.

Prayer that leads toward forgiveness simply asks God's blessing on the survivor's partner.

Period.

Amen.

Stop talking.

She doesn't get to tell God what kind of blessing to give.

"Todd," a recovering alcoholic, suggests praying for God to provide the other person with all the blessings the pray-er knows God wants for him. It's a pretty extravagant prayer, and entirely appropriate. God knows best what the survivor's partner—or anyone else—needs, and God knows what he is doing about it. She needs to affirm God's goodness and get herself out of the way.

Pray for God's understanding. When she feels resentful toward someone, a survivor almost invariably sees that person as being more powerful and less vulnerable than in fact he is. She also has an unfortunate tendency to downplay her own contribution to a difficult situation. A correction to this tendency is to ask God to help her see the situation as he does.

Sometimes I picture my former husband in a real setting that is painful for me, such as a children's event or a peaceful imaginary setting, like the bank of a beautiful river. I picture myself at a safe distance from him. Finally, I imagine Jesus entering the scene. I watch for where Jesus goes, and I listen for what he might have to say to both my former husband and me. Jesus' message is always different from my own. Invariably my feelings and my perspective shift.

God loves both the survivor and her former partner. God sees the vulnerability and pain they both hold. God wants her to be healed and at peace. Even if the *relationship* will never be healed, God has the capacity to heal her heart, one little bit at a time.

FORGIVENESS AND COMMUNITY

David Livingston, in his book *Healing Violent Men,* suggests that faith communities can play a role in reconciliation for abusers who acknowledge their actions, are truly sorry, and make amends.[38] South Africa's Truth and Reconciliation Commission offered amnesty to those who had committed heinous crimes if the perpetrators publicly described and took responsibility for their actions. Victims were given the opportunity to testify, to look their oppressors in the eye in the presence of the community and have the truth acknowledged.

Such a process would provide enormous relief for survivors of partner abuse. However, only a minority of couples is likely to experience such an outcome. The abuser's history of feigned contrition, intended only to avoid consequences and to keep the woman in his circle of influence, is extremely difficult to break. It is almost impossible for outsiders to know whether an abuser's statements represent true sorrow or an attempt to manipulate. However, this ideal is one to be considered. Not only could such a process, in the presence of a selected group of knowledgeable and supportive listeners, heal individual families, but it would also provide a way of addressing and diminishing the incidence of domestic abuse in the world. Communities can play a powerful role in healing both perpetrators and survivors.

Forgiveness is an ongoing process. A survivor may find forgiveness virtually impossible until she has taken back a measure of her power. While she is fighting for physical or emotional survival, it may be literally impossible to forgive. She may need to establish some boundaries and experience some healing before she will be able to progress in forgiveness.

But even though she can't *feel* progress, the survivor can consistently choose to *try* to forgive and to be respectful when she interacts with her former partner. As the saying goes, if she is paddling a canoe upstream and the current is as strong as she is, she may not be able to make headway. But she can still stop herself from heading over the falls.

She can look to others for inspiration. Dr. Martin Luther King, Jr., and members of the civil rights movement perfected a peaceful response to hatred. The hostility of racism and the hostility of abuse share a similar face. As she becomes clear about the true nature of abuse, the survivor struggles to discover how to *be* in the presence of such malice. How is she to think about her former partner, and how is she to carry herself in relation to him? Even if she does not have a relationship in terms of conversation and physical presence, there is still an ongoing emotional relationship. As long as the abuse is present to a significant degree in her thoughts, she needs to find a position in relationship to it.

Dr. King and his supporters faced down violence and hatred with deep courage and compassion. He taught his followers a *spirit* of nonviolence that formed the foundation of *actions* of nonviolence. He worked to build the "beloved community," a place where all can live with dignity. He urged people to recognize all human beings as their brothers and sisters, to hate the sin while loving the sinner.

I often asked myself what Martin Luther King, Jr., would do in a given situation. How could his teachings be translated for women who are fighting their own private civil rights battle? This may seem like a stretch, but it's not. The civil rights movement was about people standing up for themselves, demanding respect from those who did not want to give it. The civil rights movement was about power—about gaining respect by shifting an unequal balance of power between white people and people of color. The survivor's struggle is the same—to take back her power and to live with respect for herself, even when her dignity continues to be violated by an abuser.

I bought a huge book of King's best known writings, sermons, and speeches, and for over a year I read a bit each day. I was inspired by his capacity to passionately name the evil of racism while leading others toward confronting hatred with love. When I was preparing for an encounter with my former husband, I imagined King and his colleagues facing down hateful crowds and police officers with snarling dogs. The goal of nonviolence is to look hatred calmly in the eye and see the person behind the behavior. King says the love a survivor seeks is not sentimental; it does not necessarily involve warm feelings. She may or may not still have affection for her former partner, but that is not the basis for her current relationship. Her goal is neither to undercut nor to overpower her partner. Her goal is to look him in the eye with respect and without fear, standing firm in the truth of what she knows.

Psychologist Alice Miller encourages parents to be mirrors for their children. Parents, and society, are the means by which a child discovers who she is. Mirrors reveal her appearance to her. A good mirror bounces light accurately, so when she glances at it she sees a true reflection of herself. I do not have the capacity to change my former husband, but I do have the ability to be an accurate mirror for him. He can see himself in my eyes, as he is. I can look at him with compassion, while still knowing he is accountable for his choices. I can hold reality in my heart and allow it to guide my actions and frame my attitude. Forgiveness, while letting go of the partner relationship, offers a survivor firm ground to come to see her partner and herself in God's light.

Epilogue

This may have been a tough book for you to read. It was a tough book to write. But as I look back over these difficult chapters, I realize many struggles that once caused me such pain are now only dim memories. That is the miracle of recovery.

Recovering from abuse is a long and challenging process. As of this writing, I've been at it seven years. It has taken much more time than I'd hoped to invest, but I have made much more progress than I ever thought possible.

Recovery requires you to come to terms with the darkness that has surrounded you. Laura, my therapist, has several images of butterflies in her office, gifts from former clients. When I asked the reason, she explained that in their cocoons caterpillars disintegrate into a formless mass before being transformed and breaking free of their prisons. Like butterflies, many of you pass through a frightening period when you seem to have lost yourself. Only then will you begin to develop the fragile but powerful wings that will carry you on to new life.

Recovery asks you to grieve, to assess your wounds, and to find the resources to heal them. Recovery also invites you to look for the rainbow emerging as the mists clear away. In the ancient Genesis story, a rainbow appears in the sky after water has flooded the earth. The beautiful arch is a sign of God's promise that such destruction will never again come to pass.

Butterflies and rainbows are not just cute decorations. They are powerful symbols for the reality that opens before you. You are stepping into a new life, a new you. You are reclaiming your soul. As you leave behind the turmoil of abuse, you open space in your life to other people who know how to love, who are generous and kind, and who have grown up.

Time alone will not heal. You have to choose recovery. Let the wisdom of scripture guide you to choose Love, and thus to choose life:

> *Surely, this commandment that I am commanding you today is not too hard for you, nor is it too far away. It is not in heaven, that you should say, "Who will go up to heaven for us, and get it for us so that we may hear it and observe it."* . . . *No, the word is very near to you, it is in your mouth and in your heart for you to observe. See, I have set before you today life and prosperity, death and adversity.* . . . *Choose life so that you and your descendents may live, loving the Lord your God, obeying him, and holding fast to him; for that means life to you and length of days* . . . *(Deuteronomy 30:11–12, 14–15, 19–20).*

By working through the chapters of this book, you have chosen life. You have wandered courageously through the desert, searching for the Promised Land. You have chosen to obey the commandment of love, and the promised new world is opening before you.

You have the opportunity to continue to find a new way to love. Society and even your heart may tell you that having a life partner is necessary to be happy, but a new primary relationship may or may not be possible. It is wonderful to share life intimately with one special person, but it is not essential. What is essential is love.

Your life has paralleled the trials of Job, who was tested by having his possessions, his family, and even his health taken from him. Tradition sees Job's victory in his refusal to curse God in the midst of his suffering. Perhaps Job's final victory was trusting God enough to start over, to embrace the new family offered him after he remained faithful through his suffering.

You are being called to trust enough to love and be loved. Love can be found in many places, and the wise learn to see love in all its forms. You can love your children, if you have them. You can love other people's children if you don't. You can love your family, friends, coworkers, and the clerk in the grocery store. You can love sunsets, music, penguins, or a cause.

You can learn to breathe deeply and live in the present. You have spent so much time looking over your shoulder or scanning the horizon ahead. It may take time to learn to relax, to really savor a cup of tea, a child's smile, a moment of leisure. But it is well worth it.

You can lean into a relationship with God. For some, God is the solace that carried them through the storm. Their faith has never wavered. For others, turmoil has rocked their faith. Their sense of God, at least on an emotional level, is often shaped by their experience of life. It can be hard to trust God when life is treating you badly, but you can learn to find him in suffering and in joy.

Author Frederic Luskin, in his book *Forgive for Good*, speaks of the importance of story.[39] Your story is the way you describe yourself and your experiences to yourself and others. As you move forward you need to rewrite your story. Whenever you first began to tell your story to others, the focus was on the abuse you experienced. You could legitimately describe yourself as a victim. Becoming free of the past includes changing your story to seeing yourself as a hero. You are transcending and transforming the difficult experiences of your past. As time passes, lessons emerge, and compassion grows. You are a survivor, and the story you tell yourself and others needs to reflect that reality.

Even with the miracle of healing, you will continue to be vulnerable. There may be certain stressors—people who cross boundaries, intense conflict, persistent fatigue—that you simply must avoid whenever possible. People with heart conditions can lead normal lives, but they need to take specific steps to protect their health. You have your own kind of heart condition. Your life can be normal in many ways, but you will need to protect yourself for the rest of your days from certain difficulties.

Even with the best of intentions and support, you may falter and stumble into the darkness from time to time. While discouraging, these moments do not need to become permanent. You can learn from each episode and move on, stronger in recovery.

If you have children, the dynamics in your family will probably continue to shift, sometimes in unexpected and disheartening ways. A nonrecovering abuser may continue to disrupt your children's lives and use the children to disrupt yours. There may continue to be losses you had not anticipated. But you have learned how to absorb and transform them. You may find you weep easily, but you don't have to cry for long. You can learn to stay balanced, and your serenity can spread to your children.

Each survivor's epilogue is unique. You have your own history, personality, and circumstances. You will write your own epilogue—your story. The outcome will probably surprise you. In five years, when you look back at this point, you will shake your head in wonder that you and your life could change so dramatically.

To get there, you must settle into the deepest wisdom of your heart. You can look at the horizon and see opportunities instead of danger. You can do the same tomorrow, and the day after, and the day after. You can greet each day with gratitude: "Thank you, God, for the gift of this day. Help me to live it according to your will."

The resilience of the human spirit is amazing. The goodness of God is undeniable.

Appendix

PRINCIPLES FOR HEALTHY BOUNDARIES WHEN A RELATIONSHIP ENDS

Healthy boundaries protect everyone involved. While setting boundaries may be challenging, in the long run the benefits of good boundaries outweigh the costs for everyone.

Many people do not respect boundaries even when they are named. In these cases it may be necessary to take action to protect those boundaries. Protecting boundaries with action may be uncomfortable or even unpleasant, but it is not disrespectful or unkind. Assertive communication techniques can provide the strength and safety to maintain boundaries respectfully.

1. Relationships are best handled directly. Avoid doing the emotional or informational work of other people's relationships. Actively decline others' attempts to do the informational or emotional work of your relationships.

2. Watch for and step out of relationship triangles when possible. Relationship triangles happen when a third party gets drawn into conflict or anxiety between two people. Triangles are inherently unstable and risky. They are rarely helpful.

3. Adults have primary responsibility for taking care of themselves or securing appropriate help from others.

4. People learn best from experience. Adults need to be allowed to experience the consequences of their choices.

5. If a former partner chooses for whatever reason not to have an active relationship with another person, that decision has consequences. One of the consequences is a lack of information about that person. It is not the responsibility of a former partner to manage information about a third party.

6. It is rare for adult children to need coparenting. Most often, coparenting adult children is in fact a function of the spousal relationship:

the couple shares the joys and challenges of their experiences with their children. In healthy divorced families, relationships with adult children are almost exclusively independent of the former partner. Coparenting is required only when one parent's action directly impacts or connects with the other's (i.e., planning a wedding). Unnecessary interactions about children are a return to the old spousal relationship.

7. Allowing a boundary violation communicates permission to violate boundaries in the future.

8. Other people's behavior can be reinforced or discouraged, but it cannot be controlled.

Boundary issues occur in all relationships. Boundaries can be learned and practiced in a variety of settings. Lessons learned in one setting can be transferred to another setting. Maintaining healthy boundaries in other areas of life will have a positive impact on primary relationships.

Resources

Al-Anon Family Groups. *How Al-Anon Works for Families and Friends of Alcoholics.* Virginia Beach, VA: Al-Anon Family Group Headquarters, Inc., 1995.

————. *Paths to Recovery: Al-Anon's Steps, Traditions and Concepts.* Virginia Beach, VA: Al-Anon Family Group Headquarters, Inc., 1997.

Alberti, Robert, and Michael Emmons. *Your Perfect Right: Assertiveness and Equality in Your Life and Relationships.* Atascadero, CA: Impact Publishers, Inc., 1970.

Beattie, Melody. *Codependent No More: How to Stop Controlling Others and Start Caring for Yourself.* Center City, MN: Hazelden, 1992.

————. *Codependents' Guide to the Twelve Steps.* New York: Simon and Schuster, 1990.

de Becker, Gavin. *The Gift of Fear: Survival Signals That Protect Us from Violence.* Boston, MA: Little, Brown & Co., 1997.

Berry, Dawn Bradley. *The Domestic Violence Sourcebook.* Los Angeles, CA: Lowell House, 2000.

Bishops' Committee on Marriage and Family Life; Bishops' Committee on Women in Society in the Church. *When I Call for Help: A Pastoral Response to Domestic Violence Against Women.* Washington, DC: United States Catholic Conference, 1992.

Brewster, Susan. *To Be an Anchor in the Storm: A Guide for Families and Friends of Abused Women.* Seattle, WA: Seal Press, 1997.

Carter, Rita. *Mapping the Mind.* Los Angeles: University of California Press, 1999.

Cloud, Henry, and John Townsend. *Boundaries: When to Say Yes, When to Say No, to Take Control of Your Life.* Grand Rapids, MI: Zondervan Publishing House, 1992.

Co-Dependents Anonymous. www.coda.org.

Decker, David J. *Stopping the Violence: A Group Model to Change Men's Abusive Attitudes and Behaviors.* New York: The Haworth Press, Inc., 1999.

Doherty, William J. *The Intentional Family: How to Build Family Ties in Our Modern World.* New York: Addison-Wesley, 1997.

Donaldson-Pressman, Stephanie, and Robert M. Pressman. *The Narcissistic Family: Diagnosis and Treatment*. New York: Macmillan, 1994.

Enright, Robert. *Forgiveness Is a Choice*. Washington, DC.: American Psychological Association, 2001.

Fossum, Merle A., and Marilyn J. Mason. *Facing Shame: Families in Recovery*. New York: W.W. Norton & Company, 1986.

Friedman, Edwin H. *Generation to Generation: Family Process in Church and Synagogue*. New York: The Guilford Press, 1985.

Herman, Judith. *Trauma and Recovery: The Aftermath of Violence—From Domestic Abuse to Political Terror*. New York: Basic Books, 1997.

Kearney, Robert J. *Within the Wall of Denial: Conquering Addictive Behaviors*. New York: W.W. Norton & Company, 1996.

Kivel, Paul. *Boys Will Be Men: Raising Our Sons for Courage, Caring and Community*. Gabriola Island, BC: New Society Publishers, 1999.

———. *Uprooting Racism: How White People Can Work for Racial Justice*. Gabriola Island, BC: New Society Publishers, 1996.

Lerner, Harriet. *The Dance of Anger: A Woman's Guide to Changing the Patterns of Intimate Relationships*. New York: Harper and Row, 1985.

Livingston, David J. *Healing Violent Men*. Minneapolis, MN: Fortress Press, 2002.

Luskin, Fred. *Forgive for Good*. San Francisco: HarperSanFrancisco, 2003.

MacNutt, Francis. *Healing*. Notre Dame, IN: Ave Maria Press, 1974.

May, Gerald G. *Addiction and Grace: Love and Spirituality in the Healing of Addictions*. San Francisco, CA: Harper & Row, 1988.

Mellody, Pia, and Andrea Wells Miller. *Breaking Free: Handbook for Facing Codependence*. San Francisco, CA: HarperSanFrancisco, 1989.

———. *Facing Codependence: What It Is, Where It Comes from, How It Sabotages Our Lives*. San Francisco, CA: HarperSanFrancisco, 2003.

Naparstek, Belleruth. *Invisible Heroes: Survivors of Trauma and How They Heal*. New York: Bantam Dell, 2004.

Paymar, Michael. *Violent No More: Helping Men End Domestic Abuse*. Alameda, CA: Hunter House Publishers, 2000.

Pollack, William. *Real Boys: Rescuing Our Sons From the Myths of Boyhood.* New York: Henry Holt and Company, 1998.

Rando, Therese A. *Treatment of Complicated Mourning.* Champaign, IL: Research Press, 1993.

Rosenberg, Marshall B. *Nonviolent Communication: A Language of Life.* Encinitas, CA: Puddle Dancer Press, 2003.

Shapiro, Francine, and Margot Silk Forrest. *EMDR: The Breakthrough Therapy for Overcoming Anxiety, Stress, and Trauma.* New York: Basic Books, 1997.

Schiraldi, Glenn R. *The Post-Traumatic Stress Disorder Sourcebook.* Los Angeles, CA: Lowell House, 1991.

King, Martin Luther, Jr. *A Testament of Hope: The Essential Writings and Speeches of Martin Luther King, Jr.* Edited by James M. Washington. San Francisco, CA: HarperSanFrancisco, 1986.

Weldon, Michelle. *I Closed My Eyes: Revelations of a Battered Woman.* Center City, MN: Hazelden, 1999.

Wink, Walter. *Engaging the Powers: Discernment and Resistance in a World of Domination.* The Powers, Vol 3. Minneapolis, MN: Fortress Press, 1992.

Wink, Walter, ed. *Peace Is the Way: Writings on Nonviolence from the Fellowship of Reconciliation.* Maryknoll, NY: Orbis Books, 2000.

Notes

1. Maya Angelou, *Wouldn't Take Nothin' for My Journey Now* (New York: Bantam Books, 1994).

2. Dawn Bradley Berry, *The Domestic Violence Sourcebook* (Los Angeles, CA: Lowell House, 2000), 7.

3. Ibid., 18.

4. Michael Paymar, *Violent No More* (Alameda, CA: Hunter House Publishers, 2000), 232.

5. Lenore Walker, *The Battered Woman* (New York: Harper and Row, 1979).

6. David J. Decker, *Stopping the Violence* (New York: The Haworth Press, Inc., 1999), 32–33.

7. Robert J. Kearney, *Within the Wall of Denial: Conquering Addictive Behaviors* (New York: W.W. Norton & Company, 1996), 12–23.

8. Michelle Weldon, *I Closed My Eyes* (Center City, MN: Hazelden Information and Educational Services, 1999), 163.

9. Berry, *Domestic Violence Sourcebook*, 191.

10. Paymar, *Violent No More*, 239.

11. Berry, *Domestic Violence Sourcebook*, 5.

12. Ibid.

13. Patricia Tjaden and Nancy Thoennes, *National Violence Against Women Survey.*

14. *Minneapolis Star Tribune,* March 19, 2000, B1.

15. *Minneapolis Star Tribune,* December 9, 2000.

16. Henry Cloud and John Townsend, *Boundaries: When to Say Yes, When to Say No, to Take Control of Your Life* (Grand Rapids, MI: Little, Brown & Co., 1997), 31.

17. Harriet Lerner, *The Dance of Anger: A Woman's Guide to Changing Patterns of Intimate Relationships* (New York: Harper and Row, 1985), 23.

18. Gavin de Becker, *The Gift of Fear: Survival Signals That Protect Us From Violence* (Little, Brown & Co.: Boston, 1997), 172–193.

19. Ibid., 128.

20. Ibid., 187.

21. W.L. Williams, J.C.D., and M.A. Zona, "Stalking: Successful Intervention Strategies," *The Police Chief* (February 1996): 24-26 (cited in brief on stalking).

22. Harriet Lerner, Ph.D., *The Dance of Intimacy: A Woman's Guide to Courageous Acts of Change in Key Relationships* (New York: Harper Perennial, 1989), 104.

23. Paul Kivel, *Uprooting Racism: How White People Can Work for Racial Justice* (Gabriola Island, BC: New Society Publishers, 1996), 67–70.

24. Judith Herman, M.D., *Trauma and Recovery* (New York: BasicBooks, 1997), 34. Doctor Herman is associate clinical professor of psychiatry at Harvard Medical School and director of training at the Victims of Violence Program at Cambridge Hospital.

25. Ibid., 161.

26. "What Is Thought Field Therapy?" from The Thought Field Therapy Training Center of La Jolla, CA website (http://thoughtfield.com/about.htm), accessed April 29, 2006.

27. Therese Rando, *Treatment of Complicated Mourning* (Champaign, IL: Research Press, 1993), 347.

28. Ibid., 393.

29. Ibid., 399.

30. Ibid., 48–50.

31. Ibid., 414.

32. Ibid., 423.

33. Ibid., 386.

34. Ibid., 9.

35. Ibid., 10.

36. Ibid.

37. Cloud and Townsend, *Boundaries*, 134–5.

38. David Livingston, *Healing Violent Men* (Minneapolis, MN: Fortress Press, 2002), 23.

39. Luskin, *Forgive for Good*.

Finding few resources for families facing domestic abuse, Connie Fourré wanted to help families understand and cope with the abuse they were experiencing. She wrote *Finding Your Way through Domestic Abuse* from her own experience and after extensive research in abuse and recovery. She is also the author of several other books, including *In Praise of Homemaking* and *Journey to Justice*, a resource for Catholic educators. Fourré holds a bachelor's degree from College of St. Benedict and a master's degree from the University of St. Thomas. She is a theology teacher and volunteers as a community educator on domestic abuse. Fourré, a mother of five, lives in Minnesota.

Finding Your Way Series

Finding Your Way through Divorce
Kathy Brewer Gorham
Written from both personal experience and research, Kathy Brewer Gorham uses an honest, yet gentle approach to minister to those facing the highs and lows of ending a marriage.
ISBN: 1-59471-074-0 / 128 pages / $10.95

Finding Your Way after Your Spouse Dies
Marta Felber
Having experienced her own spouse's death, she knows the grief readers are feeling and encourages them to give it full expression. At the same time, she offers sound, practical suggestions on how to navigate difficult days.
ISBN: 0-87793-932-2 / 160 pages / $12.95

Finding Your Way after Your Parent Dies
Hope for Grieving Adults
Richard B. Gilbert
Rev. Richard Gilbert has created a compassionate guide for those struggling with the loss of a parent. From the disorientation that can come immediately after death to healing old emotional wounds, the topics dealt with here will be of tremendous help to many.
ISBN: 0-87793-694-3 / 128 pages / $9.95

Finding Your Way to Say Goodbye
Comfort for the Dying and Those Who Care For Them
Harold Ivan Smith
Smith offers comfort and guidance on issues such as: Dealing with Privacy, Crying, Partnering with Physicians, Embracing God, Expressing Anger, Forgiving, Making a Will, Making Visitors Comfortable, and more.
ISBN: 0-87793-975-6 / 224 pages / $12.95

Finding Your Way after Your Child Dies
Phyllis Vos Wezeman & Kenneth R. Wezeman
Offers parents a comforting way to grieve whenever the need arises. The themes may be easily adapted for use in small and large group settings such as a support group, a prayer service, or a family ministry session.
ISBN: 0-87793-700-1 / 192 pages / $11.95

Available from your local bookstore or from **ave maria press**
Notre Dame, IN 46556 / www.avemariapress.com
ph: 1.800.282.1865 / fax: 1.800.282.5681
Prices and availability subject to change.